"Tom Siebel has not only built a highly successful eBusiness—he has now identified the eight powerful principles that define success in eBusiness."
—Dr. John Quelch, Dean, London Business School

"In the early days of the web, many thought eBusiness was only about automating business processes and about buying and selling things over the Internet. Tom Siebel's book reminds us that eBusiness is fundamentally about satisfying customers. That has come to mean communicating with them across multiple channels in an integrated fashion. *Taking Care of eBusiness* explains how to leverage technology to that end."
—A. Michael Spence, Dean Emeritus,
Stanford Graduate School of Business,
and Partner, Oak Hill Venture Partners

"Tom Siebel is a different breed of CEO who has not only created a superb company of dedicated professionals, but has also defined a completely new business area."
—James H. Morris, Dean, School of Computer Science,
Carnegie Mellon University

Taking Care of
eBusiness

*How Today's Market Leaders Are Increasing
Revenue, Productivity, and Customer Satisfaction*

Thomas M. Siebel

Founder, Chairman, and CEO,
Siebel Systems

CURRENCY
New York   London   Toronto   Sydney   Auckland

A CURRENCY BOOK
Published by Doubleday
a division of Random House, Inc.
1540 Broadway, New York, New York, 10036

SPECIAL SALES
Currency Books are available at special discounts for bulk purchases for sales
promotions or premiums. Special editions, including personalized covers,
excerpts of existing books, and corporate imprints, can be created in large
quantities for special needs. For more information, write to Special Market,
Currency Books, 280 Park Avenue, 11th floor, New York, NY, 10017,
or email specialmarkets@randomhouse.com.

Library of Congress Cataloging-in-Publication Data
Siebel, Thomas M.
    Taking care of ebusiness : how today's market leaders are increasing
revenue, productivity, and customer satisfaction / Thomas M. Siebel.
       p. cm.
    Includes bibliographical references and index.
    ISBN 0-385-50227-3
       1. Electronic commerce. 2. Success in business. 3. Strategic planning.
    I. Title.
    HF5548.32.8543 2001
    658.8'4—dc21   2001028413

Book design by Erin L. Matherne and Tina Thompson
Printed in the United States of America
First Edition: May 2001

10 9 8 7 6 5 4 3 2 1

CONTENTS

Few individuals are more qualified to advise organizations on the subject of eBusiness than Tom Siebel. As founder, Chairman, and CEO of Siebel Systems, Inc., Tom heads what has become the world's leading provider of customer-focused eBusiness applications software. Founded in 1993, Siebel Systems surpassed $1.7 billion in annual revenue just seven years later—making it the fastest-growing software company in history. Its roster of customers reads like a who's who of the world's best-known brands, and Siebel Systems now holds a commanding market share in virtually every segment in which it competes. Analysts regard it as one of the world's best-managed firms.

Taking Care of eBusiness is refreshing and instructive because it is based on Siebel Systems' participation in more than 2,000 implementations of eBusiness systems throughout the world. Informed by this broad range of experience, Tom Siebel defines the eight essential principles of eBusiness and explains how to implement those principles. Tom shows, through real-world examples, how today's eBusiness pioneers are applying technology to get closer to their customers, improve the quality of the customer experience, and increase customer satisfaction.

Most books about eBusiness focus primarily on the Internet as a channel for buying and selling goods and services. Tom, in this book, and Siebel Systems as a company keep the customer center stage. This customer focus has been the secret to Siebel Systems' success, and this book guides organizations in how they can harness technology to create strong, lasting relationships with their customers.

Certainly the Internet has changed the way organizations do business. But its greatest impact has been to expand further the channels by which customers interact with organizations. Customers now have multiple ways to find information about products and services, to communicate with organizations, to purchase goods and make other transactions, and to receive support; and today's customers demand more choice in how they interact with organizations, not less. The business world has become increasingly *multichannel,* and organizations require new technologies and processes to meet the challenges of this new reality.

According to Tom Siebel's vision, articulated throughout this book, the purpose of eBusiness is to leverage information and communication technology to identify, acquire, and retain loyal, profitable customers more effectively. Not only can today's customers choose from an increasing number of providers offering more products and services, they also have the means to act upon those expanding options with unprecedented ease and speed. Organizations must therefore respond by being able to conduct business with customers at any time or place, in any language or currency, and through any distribution or communication channel. The greatest challenge is to maintain a seamless, one-to-one dialogue with customers as they randomly traverse channels, to recognize the customer at every moment of the conversation, and to capture information about customers at every point of their interaction with the organization.

Taking Care of eBusiness provides a tested prescription for meeting this challenge: a multichannel eBusiness system—such as those described in this book—that enables organizations to track all these interactions and leverage the captured information. This eBusiness model is designed and has been proven to produce concrete results: demonstrable increases in revenue, productivity, and customer satisfaction. *Taking Care of eBusiness* bases the development of a successful eBusiness strategy on eight fundamental principles—the first of which is to know your customer—and provides a succinct five-step methodology for devising, planning, and deploying an eBusiness strategy. With this road map in hand—a highly pragmatic, action-oriented approach to identifying opportunities for quick wins, rapid implementation, and adjustment—any organization can begin to make the eBusiness transformation.

No organization can take its customers for granted—a timeless truth that is more urgent today than ever before. Even an organization's most loyal customers are increasingly vulnerable to the allures of the competition. By following the principles spelled out in this book, all organizations—regardless of industry, size, or location—can take proactive measures to protect their existing customers from competitors and more effectively acquire and retain additional profitable customers.

Henry M. Paulson, Jr.
Chairman and CEO
The Goldman Sachs Group, Inc.

Taking Care of
eBusiness

PART I

eBusiness for a Customer-Driven World

CHAPTER ONE

What Is eBusiness?

M uch of the current discussion surrounding eBusiness creates more confusion than clarity. A large part of that confusion stems from the widespread misconception that eBusiness simply means buying and selling products and services over the Internet. As I will to try to make clear, the practice of eBusiness is not limited to the Internet, nor does it simply involve online commerce.

On the contrary, eBusiness entails the strategic use of information and communication technology (including, but not limited to, the Internet) to interact with customers, prospects, and partners through multiple communication and distribution channels. By providing the capability to both capture and manage information from these multichannel activities, eBusiness enables organizations to derive maximum value from every interaction and to continuously improve the quality of the customer experience.

The principles and methodology of eBusiness that I discuss in *Taking Care of eBusiness* are based on the actual experiences of hundreds of organizations that have implemented eBusiness capabilities. References to dozens of these organizations—most of which we at Siebel Systems, as the world's leading provider of eBusiness application software, have worked with—appear throughout the pages that follow. The reasons these organizations have pursued eBusiness are straightforward: to improve employee productivity, increase revenue, and maximize customer satisfaction, thereby increasing customer loyalty, retention, and profitability.

Early adopters of eBusiness recognize that in today's environment, the key source of competitive advantage is the ability to deliver a consistently satisfying experience to the customer. By contrast, organizations historically competed primarily by differentiating themselves on the basis of product features and functionality, price, or geographic availability. Today, however, organizations' ability to differentiate themselves based on those factors is declining. Competitors quickly imitate innovations in product features, and competing on price is, for most sellers, simply a prescription for eroding profit margins. In addition, as industries from aircraft to financial services to telecommunications are subjected to greater global competition, geographic location is an increasingly irrelevant basis of differentiation. Today, therefore, organizations are finding that competitive strategy must focus on the customer, and the key differentiators for competitive success are ease of doing business and recognized leadership in providing superior customer satisfaction.

Many factors are driving organizations to pursue this customer-focused approach to competitive strategy. Among them:

- mounting pressure on producers to compete on price—despite the unsustainability of price-based competition—which makes service-based differentiation all the more important
- the availability of technologies that enable organizations to unify customer interactions across all channels—technologies that include the Internet; remote databases; computer-integrated telephony; cell phones that are able to access Web pages by using Wireless Application Protocol (WAP); and so on
- the growing availability and organizations' expanding use of complementary, cost- and time-effective channels (e.g., resellers, call centers, the Web)
- the fact that spending of information technology funds on solving the Y2K problem is over, thus freeing IT budgets to focus on increasing the quality of the customer experience
- the proven return on investment of early adopters of eBusiness capabilities

The cumulative effect of these factors is a new reality, characterized by heightened competition, an enormous increase in the speed and complexity with which business must be done, and rising pressure on organizational leaders to find solutions to these key challenges. Reflecting this new reality, boardrooms and executive offices everywhere are filled with debates at the highest levels, centered on one question: How can we transform our organization into an eBusiness? Organizations of every size, on every continent, and in every industry are engaged in this sober introspection.

In a recent report titled *E-business: Opportunities, Threats, and Paper Tigers,* for example, market research firm GartnerGroup reported: "Around the globe, managing directors, CEOs, CIOs, and vice presidents of strategic planning are asking serious e-business questions. . . . These are deadly serious questions showing concern over enterprise survival. What our clients have been telling us is that the pressure is on, and it is enormous."[1]

These concerns over survival, GartnerGroup observed, boil down to four pressing questions that business leaders are asking themselves:

- "Why are business models going to change in my industry?"
- "What does this mean to my company?"
- "When do I need to be ready?"
- "How do I get there from here?"[2]

Yet few organizations are able to answer these questions. Witness, for example, the explosion of eBusiness courses at the world's leading business schools (even mainland China's universities now offer eBusiness courses) and the proliferation of magazines such as *Business 2.0, eCompany Now, Fast Company, The Industry Standard, The Red Herring, Upside,* and *Wired*—all filled with articles and advice about eBusiness. At the same time, virtually every business analyst and scholar, as well as the editors of publications such as *Business Week, The Wall Street Journal,* and *The New York Times,* identifies eBusiness as one of the most significant factors driving change in how organizations must compete.

The first wave of eBusiness, which gained momentum in the latter 1990s, really had more to do with eCommerce than eBusiness. The rise of "dot-coms" (primarily business-to-consumer) took center stage, and a frenzied search for eCommerce riches ensued. While a handful of notable exceptions emerged with sustainable eCommerce business models, today the landscape is increasingly littered with dot-com failures. Recent victims include, for example, Pets.com, Value America, the Disney-backed Toysmart.com, online boutique Violet.com, arts and crafts purveyor Craftshop.com, London-based fashion e-tailer Boo.com, teen-entertainment site DEN.com, Viacom-backed educational toy seller RedRocket.com, home furnishings e-tailer PuertaBella.com, and appliance e-tailer Brandwise.com, which was backed by Hearst Corporation, Whirlpool Corporation, and Boston Consulting Group. A partial list of those that appear near collapse includes DrKoop.com and KBKids.com. "Internet mania," *Fortune* magazine recently declared, "has finally, decisively, burned itself out."[3] Indeed, Forrester Research, a leading surveyor of the eCommerce scene, recently predicted that more than half of all Internet retailers online today will be out of business by the end of 2001—a prediction, it appears, that is now coming true.

Now the second wave of eBusiness is upon us, and attention is shifting from Internet-centric eCommerce to customer-centric, multichannel eBusiness. This second wave is being led by organizations such as Chase Manhattan, The Dow Chemical Company, IBM, Marriott International, and WorldCom—organizations that have been busy mastering the challenges of a world increasingly defined by one dominant fact: customers are in control.

Organizations that excel at eBusiness never lose sight of one basic fact: the fundamental objective of every organization is to profitably acquire and retain customers. Nothing about eBusiness changes that essential truth. Business begins and ends with customers. Without them, an organization simply has no business—with or without the "e."

The approach described in this guide, therefore, places the customer at the center of eBusiness strategy. Reduced to its essence, the point of eBusiness is to leverage information and communication technologies to make it easier, more pleasant, and increasingly valuable for customers to do business with your organization—in any way the customer wants—and, at the same time, to maximize the value of every customer interaction. By following the principles and methodologies outlined in this guide, organizations can develop eBusiness strategies that offer a rapid and high return on investment—results that have been measured and verified by independent research.

This view differs from the usual accounts of eBusiness in three main respects. One, it focuses on the key processes that directly enhance revenues—namely, customer acquisition and retention through sales, marketing, and service. Two, it operates from the basic assumption that the customer relationship is the most critical asset of any eBusiness model. And, three, it acknowledges a reality that many eBusiness proponents fail to recognize—namely, that eBusiness is not limited to the Internet. Indeed, highly successful organizations understand that eBusiness applies to all aspects of the customer relationship and to every customer interaction, across all channels, whether online or offline. In other words, eBusiness is customer-centric, not Web-centric.

But successful organizations have always tended to be more customer-centric than their less-successful competitors. What, then, is singularly new and different about eBusiness versus traditional business? In contrast to conventional business, eBusiness enables organizations to:

Record, measure, update, and analyze (in real time) large amounts of finely detailed, customer-specific information. Organizations can now capture the minutiae of every customer interaction, including, for example, details of how and where the interaction originated, the nature of the interaction (e.g., inquiry, service request, purchase, etc.), products or services discussed or purchased, and so on. They can record the "clickstream" data of visitors to a Web site, noting, for example, how long a visitor viewed a certain Web page, the order in which a visitor accessed pages on the site, and whether the visitor abandoned a transaction before completing it. Organizations can also add externally procured data—such as data bought from a third-party information broker—to their customer database, in order to enhance their understanding of customers. Real-time analytical tools enable organizations, for example, to detect patterns in the response to an online promotion—and to modify the promotion in real time based on that analysis.

Coordinate and personalize all interactions with customers, prospects, and partners—over time, across communication channels, and across all functional areas and lines of business within the organization. As organizations expand the channels by which they communicate with customers, prospects, and partners, they face the challenge of coordinating and personalizing interactions with those constituents. With eBusiness capabilities, organizations can synchronize their interactions and maintain a personalized dialogue with each constituent, even as those interactions move from channel to channel over time.

Program "intelligence" into every customer-facing process and optimize these processes. The technology of eBusiness enables organizations to specify powerful, complex rules based on rich customer information. Organizations can apply these rules, for example, to analyze incoming inquiries and route them—whether by phone, Web, e-mail, or other channel—to the best available customer service agent for the type of inquiry, thereby improving customer service while making most efficient use of service resources.

Practice intimate, one-to-one, relationship-based marketing, sales, and service. In contrast to mass-marketing approaches to communicating with prospects and customers—in which interactions tend to be transaction-oriented—eBusiness enables organizations to establish truly one-to-one relationships with prospects and customers. The eBusiness-enabled organization remembers its past interactions with customers—no matter when or in which channel they occurred—and makes this information available to all customer-facing personnel and processes. Organizations can use this customer-specific information to tailor communications, offerings, products, and services to match individual preferences.

Execute an optimized, integrated, ROI-based (return or investment-based) system of multichannel marketing, sales, and service. Because eBusiness capabilities enable organizations to monitor, measure, and track every customer interaction, organizations are able to determine the precise results of those interactions and therefore calculate the return on every marketing, sales, and service effort. Indeed, with eBusiness capabilities, organizations can determine the profitability of each customer or account, and thereby adjust their allocation of resources to each customer based on that customer's profitability. By extending this capability across all communication and distribution channels, an organization can optimize its business model. That is, it can reach the right customers and prospects through the right channels at the right time with the right product or service—while simultaneously ensuring that its marketing, sales, and service resources are deriving maximum value from every customer interaction, and that it is investing neither too little nor too much in efforts to acquire and retain customers.

In practice, an organization achieves these capabilities by deploying a seamlessly integrated family of sales, marketing, and customer service software applications across all channels: field sales and service, call centers, resellers, the Internet, and so on.

This creates a "closed-loop" system of capturing, organizing, and leveraging detailed information about customers, prospects, and partners, so that every customer-facing employee and process operates from the same comprehensive store of logically centralized data: the right hand always knows what the left hand is doing. For example, a field sales representative can use her laptop to dial in to the corporate customer database before making a customer call, and find out that the customer had earlier that day logged on to the corporate Web site and spent fifteen minutes viewing several recently posted pages detailing a new product offering. Armed with this information, the rep can review the latest positioning information about the new product and prepare a tailored presentation.

Before the advent of the complete suite of eBusiness technologies in the late 1990s, organizations were limited in their ability to operate with such customer-focused precision. Today, the infrastructure, applications, and know-how are available for organizations to concentrate the full range of their resources on their most critical objective: to identify, acquire, and retain profitable, loyal customers.

Our Siebel *e*Business Applications, for example, enable organizations to create a comprehensive, customer-focused eBusiness system for sales, marketing, service, and partner-relationship management across all channels. The entire suite of products includes more than 140 modular applications, with vertical-market editions providing out-of-the-box customization for various specific industries, such as financial services, telecommunications, high technology, automotive, and life sciences. The applications support a broad range of operating environments and devices, including PCs, laptops, handheld computers, and cell phones.

More than 2,000 customers worldwide have implemented Siebel eBusiness Applications, and their experience provides compelling evidence of how eBusiness capabilities directly translate into substantial increases in revenues, customer satisfaction, employee productivity, and shareholder value. A recent independent survey of our customers demonstrated average increases in productivity of 21 percent; in customer satisfaction of 21 percent; and in revenues of 16 percent—all in a period of less than ten months.

eBusiness produces these dramatic results by aligning an organization's people, processes, and technology into an integrated system that enables the organization to learn about its customers, understand their needs, and develop close, long-term relationships with them. With a comprehensive eBusiness system, organizations synchronize their interactions with customers across all channels and every touch point. This enables the organization to optimize the use of multiple channels to market to, sell to, and service its customers. The result is that organizations can do business in any way that customers want—anytime, anywhere, in any language and any currency, and through any communications channel.

Unlike conventional organizations, an eBusiness-enabled organization can maintain a continuous dialogue with its customers (and with prospects and partners, as well)—about the selection, use, enhancement, and replacement of products and services—without interruption. As the dialogue progresses over time, and even as the customer randomly bounces from channel to channel—from the Web, to the call center, to the store, and back to the Web, for instance—each channel picks up the communication where it left off. From the customer's perspective, the experience is easy, pleasant, seamless—and effective.

CHAPTER TWO

eBusiness, Not eCommerce

While eCommerce—the buying and selling of products and services over the Internet—is an important component of eBusiness, it is just one element, and not necessarily the most important element. In the United States, for example—one of the earliest among all nations to adopt the use of eCommerce—online sales of retail goods to consumers in the first quarter of 2000 amounted to $5.3 billion, less than 1 percent of the total consumer retail sales of $748 billion during the quarter. Even in sales of books, for example—a category where eCommerce has made impressive inroads—the online share in 1999 was just 5.4 percent.

This is not to downplay the prospects of eCommerce. On the contrary, online sales in many categories are growing at blinding rates, and in some segments—airline tickets and stocks, for instance—it's perhaps likely that the Internet will prove to be the preferred channel for most buyers in the future. But even in these markets there will likely always be a variety of channels: some travelers, for example, will want the services of travel agents to help book a trip, and some investors will prefer to buy stocks through a trusted broker. And this will be true with virtually any product or service. Ford Motor Company, for example, will not abandon its very successful global network of dealers, though it is dramatically expanding its channel reach through call centers and service centers. It also is broadening its distribution through its own Internet activities as well as its participation in multivendor online sales channels. Ford even recently experimented with using a dynamic-pricing approach to selling cars over the Internet, via a relationship with Priceline.com, operator of the leading online "reverse auction" (in which buyers name the price that they are willing to pay and the seller then elects or declines to accept the offered price).

As powerful and compelling a medium as it is, the Internet represents another channel—albeit one that is revolutionizing the way business is conducted. Every organization must include the Internet in the way it does business: at the very least, it must use the Internet to establish a two-way communication with its customers. For most organizations, however, the Internet does not replace existing channels but adds more channel options to the mix—Web, e-mail, virtual private networks, online auctions, etc. This is because customers insist on a choice of channels. They want to be able to do business in any way that is most convenient at that moment. In banking, for example, customers want the option of going into a local branch to buy a cashier's check, calling a customer service line to inquire about a loan, using an ATM to get cash, or going online to check their statement. Every major bank must offer all of these channels if it is to compete for today's demanding customers.

Similarly, in business-to-business relationships, customers demand a choice as well: a corporate buyer of computer hardware who is planning a major purchase from Compaq Computer Corporation, for example, wants to meet with a field sales representative to work out the details; but for more routine purchases, the buyer may prefer to place an order over the Web or through a local reseller. And for after-sale support and service, the customer will use a variety of channels—the Web, e-mail, and call center—to communicate with Compaq's helpdesk.

Even in the realm of "pure" eCommerce, it's important to remember that the customer relationship does not begin and end with the online session. Typically, an organization must engage in considerable activity offline, both before and after the online transaction, to build relationships with prospects and customers. For instance, it must communicate its marketing message and value proposition, often through the use of offline channels, and must support the sale after it occurs. Amazon.com, for instance, operates two large call centers that enable prospects and customers to call with questions about products, service, orders, and so on. The centers currently do not take orders, but they play a key role in Amazon's customer-relationship strategy—and CEO Jeff Bezos recently acknowledged that customers soon will be able to order books by phone. "It's nice to get things done when you are in a taxicab, a doctor's waiting room, or an airport terminal," Bezos told *Newsweek* magazine. "Voice is a particularly good way to interact while on the run."

And consider Siebel client Yahoo!, another quintessential dot-com. As a leading Internet media company, Yahoo! caters to several constituents, but nearly all of its revenues come from a large base of advertising customers and marketing partners. Yahoo! builds and maintains these relationships by using state-of-the-art eBusiness technology to coordinate how its marketing, sales, and service departments interact with key advertisers and partners—in person, by phone and fax, over the Web, and via e-mail.

In the rush to become eBusinesses, many organizations have misguidedly assumed that this meant setting up a Web site to transact business over the Internet. But in many cases, organizations failed to coordinate and align their Web channel with their other channels and business processes. All too often, this lack of coordination has resulted in negative customer experiences—and, ultimately, lost customers. Consider the actual experience of one online shopper, who received an e-mail promotion from a leading online vendor of music CDs during the 1999 holiday shopping season. The online vendor offered to express ship all orders, if received by a certain date, for the regular shipping charge. The shopper, a frequent customer of the CD site who enjoyed its rich content, eagerly acted on the offer and ordered several items—only to be notified by an e-mail order confirmation that the items would be shipped by regular ground service. The shopper immediately sent an e-mail to inquire about the shipping status—why ground, rather than two-day express, as promised in the earlier e-mail offer? An e-mail response came quickly—it was a canned reply with no answer to the question, but with a toll-free customer service number to call. When the shopper called the number, the call center representative had no knowledge of the original e-mail promotion and was ultimately unable to satisfy the shopper. Result: one very angry ex-customer who has told that story to dozens of friends and acquaintances—not the kind of word of mouth that organizations hope for. (The ex-patron still visits the site to view its content, but orders CDs from a competitor.) The truth is, every day legions of customers—business and consumer alike—have similar experiences with eCommerce processes that are not aligned with the rest of the organization's processes.

Indeed, in the second wave of eBusiness, many organizations are rethinking how to use the Internet channel to their best advantage. Jeans maker Levi Strauss, for example, recently decided to discontinue using the Web to sell its products directly to consumers. "We are great at creating product, and creating image for the product, but our core capabilities are not the transaction and fulfillment side," Levi CEO Philip Marineau recently stated in a keynote address at "Apparel CEO Summit," an event sponsored by *Women's Wear Daily* publisher Fairchild Publications. "We know retailers that have that capability, in fact are brilliant at it, and we are going to sell online with our retail partners." Now Levi uses its Web presence to communicate with consumers about its product and to support its retail partners such as JCPenney and Macy's, directing shoppers to both retailers' stores and online sites.

Similarly, grocery-chain operator Whole Foods Market recently shut down its wholepeople.com site and merged its Internet operations into a marketing partnership with Gaiam, an online health-foods merchant. GartnerGroup detects a trend here: it projects that over the next five years, some 60 percent of all direct-to-consumer Web sites formed in the last few years will dissolve. "Ultimately," the firm predicts, "the strongest retailers to emerge will be the hybrid companies—that is, those combining several sales channels, including brick-and-mortar and Internet stores."

CHAPTER THREE

The New Competitive Reality

Why are organizations feeling such urgency about eBusiness—and why, as GartnerGroup observed, is survival the issue? The answer, in a word, is *competition*. Multiple forces are converging in the current environment to produce a new reality characterized by unprecedented levels of competition. Primary among those forces is the radical shift of power from sellers to buyers.

Customers Are in Charge

Customers are more empowered today than ever before: customers increasingly write the rules. Two main factors contribute to this new reality. First, customers are no longer at a disadvantage to sellers when it comes to information: customers today have easy access to extensive information about products, prices, quality, availability—even manufacturer and distributor costs. Second, customers can quickly discover what the alternatives are, and—whether through a call to a toll-free number, a visit to a store down the street, or the click of a mouse—they can switch to the competition with unprecedented ease.

The Internet has accelerated the trend toward greater customer empowerment. Consider, for example, today's marketplace for personal electronics. In just a few minutes, an Internet-savvy consumer can search the Web using a free online intelligent-shopping agent such as mySimon.com and find the lowest-cost vendor of virtually any electronics product. Even in product categories in which the Web is not a significant selling channel, it is profoundly altering the way customers shop for products. For example, market-research firm J. D. Power and Associates reported that in 1999, some 40 percent of new-car buyers in the United States used the Web to research their purchase, though fewer than 2 percent actually used the Web to initiate the purchase. J. D. Power expects that during 2001, more than 65 percent of United States car buyers will use the Internet to shop for a vehicle—an estimate that may be conservative: in the first quarter of 2000, GM found that 80 percent of its customers researched their purchase over the Internet before buying.

The World Is Oversupplied but Underserviced

Switching to the competition is made all the easier because, over the last few decades, the world has become oversupplied. Across nearly every industry, producers have increased capacity while simultaneously raising standards of quality and efficiency. With so many competitors offering products with similar features and quality, customers can effectively bargain with sellers as never before.

But though the world is oversupplied, it is also underserviced. That is to say, during the last few decades most producers fervently focused on optimizing their production capabilities and operational efficiency, while placing relatively little emphasis on understanding and serving customers better. The primary focus was on lowering costs: organizations optimized their operations not to maximize customer satisfaction but to minimize costs.

In many industries, therefore, producers have reached parity in their cost structures, operating efficiencies, and product features and quality. As a consequence, competing on cost or product features is more difficult. There is increasingly little opportunity for organizations to differentiate themselves on those dimensions.

So where can organizations find a new edge—what is the next basis of sustainable competitive advantage? As the early adopters of eBusiness technology and processes have already discovered, the new source of sustainable competitive advantage lies not in optimizing the supply chain but in leveraging the demand chain—that is, in developing superior abilities to identify, select, acquire, and retain profitable, loyal customers. "In an economy of overcapacity, in which we're producing more than we can consume," says Steve Pratt, Deloitte Consulting's Global Practice Co-leader for Customer Relationship Management, "customer relationships become the sustaining driver of the economic value of a company. Once your products become a commodity or near-commodity, then what matters most is how well you can acquire, retain, and grow customer relationships." Teri Lawver, an associate principal in McKinsey & Company's Marketing Practice, offers a similar view: "For most organizations, the primary opportunity or lever for growth lies in marketing and sales—in how the organization proactively identifies, understands, and addresses customer needs in order to profitably acquire and keep customers."

Competing for Customers

Perhaps more than any other factor keeping CEOs awake at night is the relentless insurgence of both existing and emerging competitors into formerly secure customer bases. Here again multiple forces are contributing to this situation. Just as technology has made it easier for buyers to find sellers, so too is it easier for sellers to find buyers (though not necessarily easier to acquire customers). In many markets, geography is no longer a basis of competitive advantage or disadvantage.

The Internet, of course, is accelerating the pace of competition in every industry. New entrants with new business models, for example, are quickly emerging, and they are attempting to lure various customer groups away from established providers. One of the most prominent examples is Amazon.com's entry into the bookselling business. Given Amazon's recent difficulties—including its need to lay off part of its workforce and the dramatic collapse of its stock price—the ultimate success of this online pioneer is uncertain. Nonetheless, Amazon's ability to disrupt an entire industry—forcing the established incumbents to assume a defensive position—has CEOs everywhere looking over their shoulders, wondering if their industry is the next to be "amazoned."

A more compelling example of the power of the Internet is Dell's success in selling computers direct to customers over the Internet, accounting for more than 40 percent of the company's revenues. Dell's ability to generate above-average profits by operating with a dramatically lower cost structure—due to the reduced selling costs of the Internet channel—has significantly changed the industry's economic dynamics. Virtually every other major PC vendor is now struggling to find a viable basis for sustainable competitive advantage against the Dell model. (It is important to note, however, that Dell's success critically depends on its multichannel strategy: in addition to its aggressive use of the Internet, the company fields an extensive direct sales force, mails millions of catalogs targeted to different segments, and employs call centers for both sales and service.)

Deregulation, Privatization, Globalization, and Technological Innovation Are Adding to the Competitive Pressures

The Internet is not the only source of increased competition. In many industries—most notably telecommunications, financial services, energy, and transportation—deregulation is the key driver of eBusiness urgency. In telecommunications, for instance, deregulation on a global scale—coupled with a flurry of technological innovation stimulated by the deregulated environment—has transformed an industry once characterized by slow-moving monopolies into one of the world's most competitive and fast-paced industries. Telecommunications firms the world over are finding that they must quickly develop eBusiness capabilities or risk being at a competitive disadvantage. In this newly competitive environment, telecommunications firms must focus on marketing, sales, and service in order to compete for customers who now have a choice of provider.

For example, in the United States, regional phone companies once enjoyed virtual monopolies for local phone service. Now those monopolies are under attack, both from established companies such as AT&T—which is using its newly acquired cable systems to offer local phone service in a growing number of markets—and from start-ups.

In the public sector, government agencies are feeling pressure from citizens, lawmakers, and other stakeholders to deliver better service. Hence these agencies are beginning to view their constituents as customers, which is stimulating a growing interest in eGovernment. Competitive pressures are also coming into play. In the United States, for example, the United States Military Traffic Management Command—a government agency that provides global transportation services to the military—was losing customers to commercial providers. Several factors contributed to this defection: for instance, the MTMC limited its service channels to the phone and in-person service at MTMC offices, and it did not have a single, integrated system for tracking and managing customer interactions. To improve its position versus these competitors, the MTMC recently installed our eBusiness software to unify and streamline its service operations—thus enabling the MTMC to deliver world-class customer service through multiple channels, including the Internet—and the agency has committed itself to providing total customer satisfaction. With the new system, for example, the MTMC is creating customer profiles, which each functional area within the command can share: this will enable every customer support representative to access customer data, including, for instance, information about previous problems and the solutions offered. In addition, representatives will have access to a centralized database of detailed support information, so that customers receive consistent information no matter which representative responds to their inquiry.

Globalization is another major force that exposes organizations to greater competition. Here, too, the Internet is quickening the pace at which geographic limits to business are being wiped away. Multinational organizations, of course, have operated on a global basis for decades. But with the Internet, the smallest organizations can now maintain an online global presence, enabling even the corner mom-and-pop shop to reach international customers. For example, HotHotHot—a popular specialty-food site on the Web—started out as a single store in Pasadena, California, and now sells its hot sauces, salsas, and other products to a growing roster of customers around the world. Though its physical presence is limited to a single site in the United States, its virtual presence is global. Whether business-to-business or business-to-consumer, organizations of every size and in every industry are thus extending their ability to engage with customers across international boundaries. In addition, organizations are accelerating and broadening their alliances with international partners, such as the partnership between British Telecom and AT&T in international telecommunications. At the same time, transnational mergers and acquisitions—such as the Chrysler–Daimler-Benz and the Rhône-Poulenc–Hoechst AG (now Aventis) combinations—are also picking up pace. As these trends fuel even greater competition in local, regional, and global marketplaces, organizations are driven to expand their market reach even further—thus creating an escalating cycle in which more globalization begets more competition, which in turn begets more globalization.

Innovations in technology similarly are driving a cyclical process that heightens competition—as can be seen, for example, in recent trends in telecommunications. The introduction of wireless technology in the early 1980s triggered a mobile communications revolution, which launched service providers on a bidding war for customers that continues to this day. The explosive emergence of the Internet in the mid-1990s fueled a frenzy of innovation aimed at providing high-speed Internet connectivity, including DSL (digital subscriber line), cable modem, and various wireless technologies. Not only are traditional telecommunications providers such as AT&T and MCI WorldCom engaged in the battle to win customers' high-speed business; numerous start-ups also have entered the fray—outfits such as broadband wireless provider Teligent, as well as Covad, NorthPoint, and Rhythms (all providers of high-speed DSL technology). Indeed, the less-familiar names now outnumber the incumbents. The telecommunications competitive landscape is forever changed by these technology-driven forces.

Customer Expectations Are Rising

Adding even more fuel to the competitive fires is the fact that customer expectations are rapidly rising. Increasingly, for example, customers are demanding more speed (e.g., faster delivery of goods), greater convenience, better economic value, and extensive self-service capabilities.

One main effect of the Web on customer behavior is that it conditions customers to expect certain features or capabilities from every organization with which the customer interacts. For example, if the customer's bank enables her to view her account statement online twenty-four hours a day, then that customer naturally expects her credit card company (and mortgage lender, and insurance company, and telephone company, etc.) to offer the same capability. That is, Web-based innovations in one industry raise customer expectations for similar innovations in other industries. The transfer of product and service innovations across industries is not new, but in the era of eBusiness it happens much faster.

Customer expectations also are rising in another important respect: the demand for personalized interactions. Increasingly, customers insist on the ability to carry on a continuous dialogue with organizations with which they do business—they want these organizations to know them in the way that local shopkeepers know their customers. Customers expect organizations to maintain a "customer memory," so that customer information—preferences, service requests, past complaints, purchases, and so on—can be leveraged across the entire organization to the customer's benefit. Each time a regular customer at a local shop comes in, for example, that customer does not have to reintroduce herself and explain her preferences all over again. Few large organizations, however, excel at this sort of customer memory.

Take, for example, the recent experience of one frequent traveler at a deluxe hotel chain: on three successive visits to the same hotel, each just a month apart, the desk clerk asked if it was her first visit—making the guest feel like an anonymous commodity and totally unappreciated. By contrast, one of our clients, Marriott International, a leading hotel and resort operator, employs a sophisticated eBusiness system to store detailed customer data in a unified database accessible by all customer-facing employees. As a result, Marriott is able to acknowledge its repeat customers as special guests and to accommodate their individual preferences based on information gleaned from their past stays and other interactions.

Industry Consolidation Adds to the Confusion

Also contributing to the mounting pressures that organizations face are the adverse effects on customer relationships caused by the consolidation that is occurring in many industries. Following a merger or acquisition, customers of the acquired or merged organization often find themselves in a state of suspended animation, as the new organization struggles to integrate these customers into its primary processes and systems. Customers are often confused or annoyed by the new arrangement: the parent company, for example, may send multiple bills—each for a separate product or service from its multiple lines of business, and each of which has to be paid and returned to a unique address—while what the customer really wants is a single consolidated bill. This makes many customers vulnerable to defection, particularly if a competitor aggressively tries to capitalize on the opportunity with special offers and promotions targeted at these susceptible customers.

Compounding the problem is the possibility that the postmerger organization may also be experiencing considerable internal confusion as it tries to digest the acquisition. Hence, just when it must pay special attention to customers caught in the transition limbo, the organization finds itself distracted by internal matters.

For business customers caught in this postmerger disarray, the situation can be especially vexing. For example, a corporate buyer expects that one sales representative should be able to represent the newly expanded portfolio of products and services. However, due to the lack of a common system with consolidated customer information, each representative knows only his original product information: the customer derives no economies of scale as a result of the merger, and this greatly hampers the merged organization's ability to increase the breadth and depth of each customer relationship without increasing the overhead proportionally—which presumably was a fundamental premise on which the merger was financially justified in the first place.

Chase Manhattan Bank exemplifies an organization that is implementing eBusiness technology in part to unify operations inherited from various mergers and acquisitions, most notably the 1996 union of Chase and Chemical Bank that formed the current combined entity. We have worked closely with Chase on a number of eBusiness projects to link their systems. For example, Chase's commercial banking division includes several lines of business (LOB) and, as a result of various acquisitions, has numerous customer information systems that are not connected to one another. Hence, even though the different LOBs have many common customers, information about them is fragmented among the disparate systems, thereby limiting the bank's ability to deliver maximum value to each customer relationship. Using our eBusiness applications as the foundation, Chase's commercial banking division is creating a single common platform to consolidate customer information across all of its lines of business. Chase believes that this customer-focused capability will enable the organization to extend the vision that is codified in its corporate motto—"The Right Relationship Is Everything"—and to take a more strategic approach to managing its customer relationships.

As a result of these various forces—empowered customers, increasing competition, rising customer expectations, globalization, privatization, deregulation, technological innovation, and industry consolidation—organizations face mounting challenges to their ability to acquire and keep customers and to maintain brand value. In every sector of the economy and in every part of the globe, many once-illustrious brands are coming under attack: Sears in the United States, for example, and Marks & Spencer in the United Kingdom. Ironically, success in this new environment ultimately depends on an ageless concept: customer loyalty. Organizations with well-crafted eBusiness systems can dramatically improve their ability to acquire and keep loyal customers—and for most organizations, customer loyalty is essential to long-term success.

CHAPTER FOUR

The Value of Customer Loyalty

Loyal customers have always been important to an organization's long-term success. But due to the heightened competition of today's environment, customer loyalty is arguably more important—and more threatened—than ever before. Virtually every organization today faces growing assaults on its customer base by competitors. At the same time, organizations are stepping up their efforts to compete for the same new customers; this drives up the cost of acquiring customers while simultaneously diminishing the effectiveness of those acquisition efforts.

In this hypercompetitive environment, the already powerful economic benefits of retaining loyal customers are even more important. Customer loyalty expert Frederick Reichheld, of management consulting firm Bain & Company, and his colleagues studied a number of industries and found that a 5 percent increase in customer retention can increase an organization's profitability by 25 to 100 percent. Stated the other way around, an organization that sees its customer retention rate slip by 5 percent may see its bottom line drop by as much as half.

How exactly does customer retention produce such dramatic economic benefits? Research indicates that there are five key sources of benefits:[4]

First, the rate at which an organization retains customers significantly affects how much it must spend to acquire new customers. Given that it can cost five to twelve times more to acquire a new customer than to keep an existing customer, there are sizable bottom-line benefits in avoiding additional customer-acquisition costs. That is to say, the less an organization depends on deriving its revenue growth from new customers, the more efficient is its marketing spending.

Second, in many industries, loyal customers tend to increase the volume of their purchases over time: in other words, loyal customers equal increased wallet share. This may happen in several ways. The average order size may increase, for example, as the customer shifts or consolidates spending to a preferred supplier—over time, for example, a consumer will buy an increasing share of groceries at a single supermarket. Loyal customers also tend to buy more products or services from a trusted provider: as they learn more about the organization's product line, they purchase additional products. For example, a holder of a car insurance policy may later secure property and life insurance policies from the same provider. Organizations, therefore, can use eBusiness capabilities to leverage the value of existing customers and cross-sell to gain additional wallet share, which is cheaper than the initial sale.

Third, long-term customers typically cost less to serve. They are generally more familiar with an organization's policies and processes, so they tend to ask fewer questions and consume fewer marketing, sales, and service resources than new customers and prospects. When established customers call customer service, for example, their calls often run shorter than other customers' calls, because they know whom to contact or have the information in hand that the agent needs to efficiently handle the call. In addition, established customers that are familiar with the provider's processes often will access services at off-peak hours and use self-service mechanisms more often, which lowers the cost of serving these customers.

Fourth, for virtually every organization, loyal customers are the best source of referrals. In most industries, word of mouth plays an important part in acquiring new customers, and in some industries—professional services such as law and accounting, for instance—referrals are the major source of new business. Nonetheless, far too few organizations consistently track word-of-mouth effects on their business, which means that they may not appreciate the full value of loyal customers. Unless the organization measures the impact of referrals, it cannot make optimal decisions about investments in efforts to drive greater loyalty.

Fifth, loyal customers are generally less price sensitive than other customers and are more willing to pay a premium for products and services. This is in part because loyal customers by nature tend to prefer stable, long-term relationships and are inherently less susceptible to competitors' price promotions. In addition, loyal customers tend to migrate to higher-margin products and services, because they value the additional benefits of those offerings.

Loyal customers, therefore, are generally an organization's best customers precisely because their preferences are best suited to the organization's offerings; in other words, loyal customers become so because they are the ones that most value what the organization has to offer. Organizations that understand the economic benefits of loyal customers treat them like gold and continually try to learn more about them. For these organizations, one of the key advantages of eBusiness is the ability to leverage information about loyal customers in order to identify and acquire more of them.

However, organizations should not automatically conclude that every long-term customer is a high-value customer; it is possible, and in fact common, that some loyal customers actually cost the organization more than they are worth. According to customer-loyalty expert Frederick Reichheld, author of *The Loyalty Effect*, "mature companies often find that 20 to 30 percent of their new customer acquisition investments should be scrapped." In banking, Reichheld maintains, "20 to 50 percent of the investments in new customer acquisition are currently directed at target groups with a negative net present value." Indeed, a study found that at one financial services organization, 20 percent of the customers accounted for more than 170 percent of the institution's profits; these customers were subsidizing losses from other customers.

This pattern persists in many industries, particularly those that involve complex product and service offerings and a high degree of customer usage variability. In the local telephone business, for example, profitability analysis reveals that at some organizations, the most valuable 10 percent of customers generate ten times as much profits as the least valuable 10 percent. Relatively few companies have performed—or are able to perform—this sort of analysis, but for those that do it is invaluable: by studying the characteristics of and soliciting feedback from these high-value customers, organizations can design programs to acquire and retain more of the same.

How, then, does an organization that understands the powerful benefits of having long-term, profitable customers translate that knowledge into strategy? This is precisely where eBusiness capabilities come into play. Properly understood and deployed, eBusiness enables the organization to leverage its information and communications technologies, build effective processes, and empower its people—all in order to focus on three related objectives:

1. identify and select prospects who are most likely to become profitable, loyal customers (based on models that can predict profitability and loyalty)
2. acquire a sufficient number of those prospects at an acceptable cost
3. retain these customers at an acceptably high rate

The success of any eBusiness strategy, therefore, depends on the organization's ability to determine:

- who is likely to become a loyal, profitable customer, by developing accurate predictive models
- how to convert these identified prospects into customers
- how to nurture these new customers, once acquired, into long-term loyalists

A fundamental objective of eBusiness, therefore, is to continuously improve the organization's understanding of its customers—that is, to get to know the customer better and better.

Having loyal customers is not an accidental result: organizations achieve high customer-retention rates through carefully planned and well-executed strategies. Successful organizations understand that the process of building customer loyalty rests on establishing strong relationships with selected customers—those that are likely to be profitable for the organization over the long run. They also understand that the dynamics of customer loyalty are self-reinforcing: as an organization learns more about its customers, it is better able to personalize its interactions with customers and tailor products and services to better suit customer needs. Then, as customers feel consistently satisfied and delighted, they escalate their relationship with the organization, and the organization learns still more about the customer from each successive interaction. The process becomes a "virtuous cycle," and the customer relationship is strengthened with each repetition of the cycle.

Long before the term "stickiness" came into vogue—referring to the tendency of Web users to return to and spend more time at favored sites—loyalty-driven organizations understood how to cement strong relationships with preferred customers to keep them coming back. In the airline industry, for example, high-frequency fliers are rewarded not only with mileage credits toward free tickets, but they also get preferential treatment in reservation handling, check-in procedures, upgrades on seating, and access to airport clubs and lounges. Though such loyalty-building efforts typically produce positive results, organizations widely recognize that in the past those efforts generally have been suboptimal, due to organizations' limited ability to record, track, and monitor the precise outcome of every customer interaction. By implementing eBusiness capabilities, however, organizations can now leverage information and communication technologies to reinforce and extend their loyalty-building efforts with unprecedented precision, thereby achieving a higher rate of customer retention—which, for most organizations, is the key difference between merely average and superior performance.

CHAPTER FIVE

eBusiness Addresses the Root Problems of Weak Customer Relationships

The typical U.S. corporation loses 50 percent of its customers every five years, reports Frederick Reichheld in his book *The Loyalty Effect*. Even more startling than that statistic, however, is the fact that few organizations actually understand why customers leave. Surprisingly, a significant percentage of customers defect not because of dissatisfaction with the basic product or price, but because they did not feel well served by the organization. In the U.S. auto industry, for example, the reason customers cite most for not repurchasing a particular brand of vehicle is a poor buying experience—not product quality, features, or price.

Why do customers so frequently feel poorly served by organizations? There are many reasons, of course—including inadequately trained personnel, customer-unfriendly processes, and an organizational culture that insufficiently emphasizes customer satisfaction—but from an eBusiness perspective, the key factor is the lack of a customer-centric architecture: organizations have typically designed their systems and processes based not on customer considerations but along product lines or internal organizational functions or divisions.

Fragmented Customer Information: The "Silo Effect"

In most organizations, customer information is typically fragmented across departments, lines of business, divisions, channels, product lines, or some other unit. The result is the silo effect: the organization has no consolidated, unified view of the customer, which can lead to a fragmented customer experience. A common story, for instance, is the credit card company whose telemarketing department, pulling information from one database, calls a prospect at dinnertime to pitch its card, not knowing that the individual already has that card—because that information resides in a different database, and the telemarketing system does not connect the two databases. Rather than serving its customers well, this company is harassing its customers. In the customer's perception, the organization regards him merely as a nameless, faceless commodity, which undermines any efforts by the organization to build customer loyalty.

By leveraging technology, early adopters of eBusiness are solving the silo effect. For example, our client Dow Chemical, a leading global science and technology company that provides innovative chemical, plastic, and agricultural products, receives thousands of customer inquiries a day, across more than fifty call centers worldwide. Information about each customer comes in from multiple channels—the Web, call centers, field sales force, technical service representatives, and e-mail. Given the sheer quantity and complexity of these interactions, Dow was concerned about missing information and not leveraging opportunities proactively.

Hoping to build customer loyalty and better share information across the various customer contact points, Dow implemented our eBusiness software to facilitate the consolidation of customer information from disparate systems and begin the creation of comprehensive customer memory. By implementing these eBusiness applications, Dow has begun to seamlessly integrate multiple contact channels and provide agents with up-to-the-minute customer information.

In another example of addressing the silo effect, we worked with a leading supplier of financial products, including mutual funds and insurance, to solve a communications problem typical of many organizations. As the company's family of business units and product lines had grown, its sales force was increasingly challenged to gather, manage, and maximize sales-related information across different groups within the organization. Barriers to effective coordination of this information included the lack of a central repository for financial representatives and insurance agents; the fact that remote users were disconnected from corporate information; and the lack of a centralized contact management platform. The sales and marketing department employed more than ten different systems to manage this information, resulting in inefficient manual processes being used to deliver summarized information to executive management. In addition, field sales wholesalers could not share information with either their in-house counterparts or with other field wholesalers who may have been approaching the same customer.

To solve the problem, the company implemented software to provide an enterprisewide eBusiness platform to integrate the sales and marketing departments of key domestic operations with its international groups. Critical to the system's success is its integration with various back-office data layers currently in production, with interface programs facilitating the exchange of information across operating units.

The system now serves as the backbone of the company's eBusiness solution to managing customer interactions, and it provides an unprecedented level of customer-information access and sharing across the entire sales organization. The company's financial advisers, representatives, and insurance agents are now able to efficiently manage contacts and prospects, track and view their activity history, and record tasks related to the sales process management, all in one central data repository. The system's state-of-the-art remote synchronization capabilities enable field personnel to exchange the most current information with the central data repository. And management now has the ability to produce up-to-date, comprehensive reports that provide a real-time view of customer relationships and sales and marketing activity.

Lack of Customer Information

At the same time, if the organization's system does not adequately capture key information about its customers, then the organization stands to miss valuable opportunities to serve its customers better, reinforce customer loyalty, and increase revenues (through appropriate cross-selling, re-selling, and up-selling efforts). The potential value of detailed customer information is illustrated by the experience of one insurance company that implemented our marketing software to create and execute a data-driven direct marketing campaign for its car insurance products. Using the software's analytic capabilities, the company discovered that a significantly large percentage of respondents to the offer were divorced women. Further analysis revealed that these customers represented an above-average risk profile—making them desirable customers—so the insurance company rolled out a highly successful campaign specifically targeted to this segment. Organizations that lack the ability to capture and analyze detailed customer information in this way obviously cannot take advantage of such opportunities.

Unsynchronized Channels

The story of the online CD shopper recounted earlier illustrates the kind of negative customer experience that can be caused by unsynchronized channels. Another typical anecdote, recounted by Forrester Research analyst Bob Chatham, concerns the experience of a Continental Airlines customer who went online to sign up for the airline's frequent flier program, Continental OnePass: "After filling out the lengthy registration form, [the] customer noticed a banner ad for seat upgrades but couldn't find the purchase location on the site. So after completing the registration—creating a PIN [personal identification number], typing identifying facts like mother's maiden name, etc.—she phoned to buy the upgrades. Since call center agents at OnePass can't see online registrations until they are posted overnight, the registration process had to be repeated over the phone."

Indeed, as organizations expand their distribution and communication channels, customers increasingly will move intermittently between channels. The problem for many organizations, however, is that they have independent structures to support each channel—a Web channel group, a call center group, a retail group—and the systems employed by each of these are not well integrated. At a leading hotel chain's Web site, for example, customers can check on the status of reservations booked over the Internet but not those made in some other way. Removing such disconnects in the customer experience and synchronizing interactions across all channels is a major objective of multichannel eBusiness.

Unintegrated, Dysfunctional Information Technology That Leads to Broken Processes

Research by the consulting firm Deloitte & Touche indicates that in the telecommunications industry, an alarming 75 percent of orders contain some sort of error. A primary cause is that large telecommunications organizations have accumulated numerous disparate ordering systems, along with multiple back-office fulfillment systems. The interfaces are often unwieldy and the systems are not well integrated. As a result, many orders are either entered incorrectly (there are few if any internal checks built into many of these antiquated systems) or are not transferred properly from system to system. Consequently, customers are frustrated by delays, incorrect billing, and the hassle of multiple service calls, while telecommunications bear the cost of expensive rework and inefficient use of resources, as well as the adverse effects of customer dissatisfaction.

By unifying ordering processes under one global eBusiness architecture with a common user interface and internal checks, organizations can dramatically reduce one of their biggest headaches. Indeed, a powerful way to reduce incorrect orders is to employ an automated configuration solution. The sales representatives at a leading provider of business-intelligence software, for example, used an unwieldy manual process to configure products and quotes for customers, which resulted in an exceedingly high percentage of incorrectly configured products. Representatives had to search through several thick manuals containing more than 40,000 part numbers to determine which products should be shipped to a customer. The company solved this problem by implementing our configurator software: part numbers are stored in a centralized database accessed via an easily navigated user interface, and the software includes rules to ensure that configurations are valid, making the whole quoting process easy and fast. As a result, because representatives could accurately select the correct part number for each quote, the percentage of misconfigured products was dramatically reduced.

CHAPTER SIX

eBusiness for the Public Sector

Though this book is written in the language of business, with frequent references to concepts such as revenues and profits, most of the eBusiness principles described here apply just as forcefully to public-sector agencies and to private nonprofits, as well. For example, we are working with organizations that include the State of Kentucky, the City of Leeds (United Kingdom), the U.K. Post Office, several U.S. armed forces agencies, the American Heart Association, and the American Cancer Society. Such organizations face many of the same forces that are driving eBusiness urgency in the private sector.

For example, while public-sector organizations do not seek to maximize customer profitability, they do attempt to maximize client satisfaction at an acceptable cost of service. Both for budgetary reasons and for reasons related to quality of service, public-sector organizations must make use of current technology to fulfill their mandates. In other words, public-sector organizations face complex optimization problems—problems that require eBusiness solutions.

In addition, many public agencies and private nonprofits must compete for resources. The all-volunteer U.S. military, for example, must compete with the private sector for qualified personnel, and therefore needs sophisticated systems to more effectively identify and acquire new recruits. Agencies ranging from the Social Security Administration to the Department of Motor Vehicles are under increasing pressure to improve the level of service to their clients. Today's citizenry, accustomed to rising standards of service in the private sector, insist on greater ease, choice, and flexibility in how they interact with public agencies. For example, they want around-the-clock access to important information, such as their Social Security account or car registration record. Internet-based self-service capabilities, for instance, would empower citizens to answer many routine questions at their own convenience, while shifting a significant share of service demands from live agents and thus freeing them to perform higher-value tasks.

Managers in the public sector, therefore, benefit from looking to eBusiness as a means to dramatically improve the level of public service while simultaneously reducing costs through greater effectiveness and efficiency.

CHAPTER SEVEN

How to Become an eBusiness

The need to embrace eBusiness is becoming increasingly obvious. With increasing urgency, organizations in every industry and in every part of the globe are recognizing that if they are to successfully compete in today's environment, they must develop eBusiness capabilities. eBusiness is not an option—it is a matter of survival. This recognition is driving the adoption of eBusiness technology at an exponential rate—a fact that has made Siebel Systems, as the world's leading provider of eBusiness applications, the third-fastest-growing company in the United States in 2000 (number one in 1999), according to *Fortune* magazine.

Nonetheless, while organizations of all types seek to become multi-channel eBusinesses and derive dramatic increases in revenues, employee productivity, and customer satisfaction, little has been written to help guide their transformation process. There is a particularly profound lack of insightful guidance based on organizations' actual experiences in making this challenging transformation. Early adopters of eBusiness have in large measure been pioneers, finding their way through a process of trial and error. The good news is that when they are dissected and examined, all of these successful projects have more commonalities than differences.

In this book I offer organizations a prescriptive explanation of eBusiness and a methodology based not on speculation or untested theory, but on the best practices of hundreds of our customers. Part II of the book explains the eight essential principles of eBusiness, which together will provide a clear framework on which organizational leaders can base their eBusiness strategy. In brief, those principles are:

1. Know your customer.
2. Use multiple channels to interact with your customers.
3. Personalize the customer experience.
4. Optimize the value of every customer.
5. Focus on 100 percent customer satisfaction.
6. Develop and maintain a global, customer-centric eBusiness architecture.
7. Leverage and extend the eBusiness ecosystem.
8. Cultivate an organizational culture based on eBusiness excellence and innovation.

As you can see, eBusiness is far more than simply deploying software. Certainly, eBusiness requires the right applications and underlying infrastructure. But it also requires the right organizational structure and processes, as well as the right focus supported by a workforce that is appropriately motivated to execute the eBusiness strategy.

Ultimately, the issue is how to use eBusiness capabilities most effectively to achieve the strategic objectives of the organization—and in eBusiness, those objectives will focus on the customer and on delivering total customer satisfaction.

Understanding the principles of eBusiness is one thing. Applying them is another. The methodology presented in Part III provides a framework for organizations to help them launch the eBusiness transformation process. It begins with identifying the organization's eBusiness strengths and weaknesses and evaluating its growth strategy. This enables the company to assess its capabilities and to define specific eBusiness objectives. Those objectives then drive various action plans, including: defining and managing the organizational change required to support the eBusiness strategy; assigning roles and responsibilities for "virtual teams" that serve customers; implementing the required technology; and monitoring, measuring, and tracking the performance of the eBusiness strategy.

eBusiness Leaders: A Closer Look

In ten case studies throughout the book, I take a closer look at the eBusiness strategies of a select group of organizations: Chase Manhattan, The Dow Chemical Company, Honeywell International, IBM, Marriott International, Nationwide Insurance, Quick & Reilly, Telstra Corporation, Threadneedle Investment Services, and WorldCom. I can write about them in particular detail because each is a Siebel Systems customer: each uses our eBusiness applications as a central component in its multichannel, customer-focused eBusiness strategy.

Representing a broad range of industries, these companies demonstrate the benefits derived from applying technology to the challenge of delivering the highest levels of customer satisfaction. Just as important, I think the experiences of these organizations provide valuable lessons and models for other companies, whatever eBusiness solutions they utilize. Whether it is IBM's concept of "broad before deep," for example, or WorldCom's "Stage 1-2-3" approach to technology deployment, each of these pioneers offers numerous insights into the successful implementation and practice of eBusiness.

While no single organization completely embodies all eight principles of eBusiness defined in this book, I have found that each of the organizations profiled here has achieved significant progress in that direction. Even more important, each has fully committed itself to becoming a customer-focused eBusiness—and in every case, that commitment has come from the highest executive ranks of the organization. The specific factors motivating each organization's pursuit of eBusiness differ from organization to organization, but the larger goal is the same for all: to deliver the highest levels of customer satisfaction.

IBM, for example—in one of the world's largest and widest-ranging eBusiness initiatives—is creating a comprehensive customer information system that will enable IBM both to present a single face to its customers and to have a single view of its customers. Through this integration, IBM will be better able to leverage its full range of capabilities to provide total solutions to its customers, maximize customer satisfaction, and ultimately capture more of its customers' business.

Two of the companies profiled—Telstra and WorldCom—operate in the telecommunications industry, but the specific circumstances driving their eBusiness strategies offer an interesting contrast. Telstra, the number-one telecommunications operator in Australia, is making the transition from state-owned monopoly to customer-centric eBusiness. The company is transforming its organizational culture and implementing eBusiness applications to help it build long-lasting relationships with its customers—which Telstra views as a fundamental necessity in the newly deregulated environment.

In contrast, WorldCom is using eBusiness applications to support its transformation from a long-distance service company to a provider of complete communications solutions. One requirement of that transformation, for example, is the ability for sales teams composed of different product-line representatives to closely collaborate on common accounts. WorldCom's Business Markets division, therefore, is using eBusiness applications to more effectively sell complete solutions and provide customer service to Global Account and National Account customers.

In the services sector, Marriott International is using eBusiness technology to support its transformation from a property-centric to a customer-centric organization. Driven by rising levels of competition and a limit on its ability to raise room rates, Marriott's strategy for revenue growth now focuses on increasing revenue per customer—that is, greater wallet share—rather than increasing revenue per room. Executing this strategy requires a highly sophisticated customer-focused eBusiness system that enables Marriott to track the preferences of each guest and to build detailed customer profiles. Marriott supports its strategy not only with technology but also with human resources practices designed to reinforce exceptional customer service.

In the manufacturing sector, two companies provide outstanding examples of eBusiness sophistication: Honeywell and The Dow Chemical Company. Honeywell is using eBusiness applications to enhance customer satisfaction and drive superior revenue growth. The $2.5 billion Honeywell Industrial Control (HIC) business unit, for example, has implemented an eBusiness system to create a knowledge repository that customers and Honeywell personnel can use to expedite problem solving. HIC has also created extranets and industry-specific Web portals to enhance customer intimacy.

At Dow, a key component of the organization's strategy involves using eBusiness technology to make Dow the easiest company in the world with which to do business, thereby leading to superior customer satisfaction, loyalty, and revenue per customer. Dow's eBusiness system is part of the company's larger effort to shift from a product-centric to a customer-centric culture. Dow's management has learned some valuable lessons from its eBusiness initiative, many of which are applicable to other organizations implementing a customer-centric eBusiness strategy.

The financial services sector has been one of the earliest adopters of customer-focused eBusiness technology: the convergence of several forces—including deregulation, consolidation, globalization, and the rise of the Internet—is fueling competition in this sector to ever-rising levels, thereby driving companies to increasingly focus on customer satisfaction as a matter of survival. Given the importance of this sector in the pioneering of eBusiness, four of the companies profiled here—Chase Manhattan, Nationwide Insurance, Quick & Reilly, and Threadneedle— compete in various financial services industries.

One of the world's largest financial institutions, Chase Manhattan is implementing a comprehensive eBusiness system to provide "the right financial solution to the right customer at the right time." A key component of the system is Chase's Customer Opportunity Management initiative, which was designed to unify all customer-facing aspects of its regional consumer banking operations. While technology plays a pivotal role in Chase's eBusiness initiative, the company also focuses significant attention on building an organizational culture that excels at eBusiness.

Nationwide Insurance, the fourth-largest automobile insurer and fifth-largest homeowners' insurer in the United States, used to store its customer information in virtual "silos," often segmented by type of policy or service. Without a common pool of customer data, Nationwide struggled to cross-sell services, deliver personalized marketing campaigns, and provide superior customer service. To overcome these challenges, Nationwide launched its "Customer Choice" initiative—a strategy that leverages eBusiness technology to help Nationwide's exclusive and independent agents grow their businesses.

Threadneedle, part of the Zurich Financial Services Group, offers mutual funds and other asset-management services to retail and institutional clients in the United Kingdom and Europe. Threadneedle has used eBusiness technology to continuously enhance its "service proposition," which has played a pivotal role in driving its exemplary performance. Threadneedle presents an excellent example of how a company can build an eBusiness system incrementally—first by using eBusiness applications to address a specific business problem, and then extending the eBusiness platform to all customer-facing channels.

In its ongoing efforts to deliver the highest levels of customer satisfaction in the brokerage industry, Quick & Reilly, a member of the FleetBoston Financial Corporation, has used eBusiness technology to develop an integrated customer-support system that gives customers the ability to move seamlessly from the Internet to the call center to a personal broker. Quick & Reilly's eBusiness system has enabled the company both to form stronger relationships with its customers and to tighten its integration with its parent company and key partners. The result is a far deeper knowledge of each individual customer and the ability to provide better service and greater flexibility to all customers.

The experiences of the eBusiness pioneers that I profile in these case studies offer, I believe, valuable lessons for all organizations, regardless of the industry in which they compete. Together, these stories provide a rich set of best practices, which I hope will pave the road to success for other organizations embarking on the eBusiness transformation. One thing is clear: developing customer-focused eBusiness capabilities is no longer an option—it is a matter of survival, and organizations must act now or risk extinction in the new economy.

PART II

The Eight Essential Principles of eBusiness

CHAPTER EIGHT

Introduction

The eight principles presented here are derived from the actual experiences of real-world organizations, representing hundreds of successful eBusiness deployments. While the adoption of eBusiness remains in its early stages, there is now ample evidence—based on the results of these eBusiness pioneers—that certain identifiable practices yield superior results. These organizations have achieved dramatic, independently confirmed increases in revenues, customer satisfaction, and employee productivity.

These principles are intended as guidelines for executives as they think about eBusiness and how it applies to their specific circumstances. Once managers appreciate the fundamental point that eBusiness is far more than setting up and transacting business over a Web site, the complex challenges of real eBusiness will become more apparent to them. By utilizing these eight principles, managers will have a systematic framework for developing a well-structured, comprehensive eBusiness strategy.

These eight essential principles identify the various objectives that managers should target. Organizations can then begin an eBusiness transformation project with several key parameters in place.

CHAPTER NINE

Principle One: Know Your Customer

Information is the lifeblood of eBusiness. The real power of eBusiness comes from the ability to capture and leverage information in order to better understand the customer and, as a result, better anticipate and serve customer needs. Without rich, detailed information about customers, an organization cannot begin to build strong customer relationships. Customer information, therefore, is key: it drives the most important decisions that an organization makes—what products and services to develop; which channels to use to bring those products and services to market; and how to communicate the value of those products and services to customers, through advertising, promotion, and other marketing activities. Therefore, the first rule of eBusiness is to *know your customer*.

Knowing your customers is not limited to knowledge of the customer's sales cycle; it also means knowing them after the sale—their service preferences, for example, and how and why they interact with your organization to find out about the use, enhancement, and repurchase of your products and services. It means knowing:

- your customer's profile and requirements
- how to match which products and services to which specific customers
- how to match resellers and other partners to meet customers' needs

- how best to provide services and support
- which marketing campaigns and offers to target to which specific customers
- how to design new products and services to meet customers' additional or changing needs
- how to reward and express your appreciation to your best customers

Furthermore, by knowing your customers in deep detail, your organization can leverage that knowledge, enabling it to precisely configure products and services to meet its customers' unique requirements and preferences.

To effectively develop this extensive scope of customer knowledge requires the application of eBusiness capabilities to systematically capture, manage, and leverage customer data. While organizations do collect considerable amounts of customer data, typically that information is never consolidated: much of it, for example, resides in the individual files or personal organizers of sales representatives, rather than captured in a fashion to be organized and shared, and upon which management decisions can be made. Ironically, then, information most important to an organization is often an *individual asset* rather than an *organizational asset*. The purpose of an eBusiness system, by contrast, is to enable an organization to systematically capture information and leverage it as a strategic asset.

First the Basics

Knowing the customer begins with collecting basic customer data. There are three general types: (1) data provided directly by the customer (e.g., information that a credit card applicant puts in the application form or a self-profile submitted on the Web); (2) transaction and interaction data that the organization captures and records (e.g., inquiries, purchases, service requests, visits to specific Web pages); and (3) data procured from third parties such as list compilers, data syndicators, credit bureaus, and other information brokers.

Precisely which basic data an organization should collect depends on the specific industry, the type of product or service being marketed, the type of customer (consumer or business), and many other factors. Typical categories of basic data include:

- demographics (income, gender, marital status, age, occupation, household composition, etc.)
- purchasing history
- geography
- industry (if a business customer)

Beyond Basic Data: Understanding the Customer Life Cycle Process

Basic data alone, however, is of limited usefulness. The real work of knowing the customer requires intense analysis, because what the organization really wants to understand is the customer's *life cycle process*—and this can only be derived from studying the data. The customer life cycle process describes how the customer actually proceeds through the entire cycle of events that lead the customer from awareness and interest in a product or service, through search and evaluation of options, to purchase and postpurchase usage, then to repurchase. Only by understanding the triggers and drivers of each of these events—the root sources of demand—can an organization truly develop a rich knowledge of its customers. And only with this information can an organization uniquely configure and price products and services to meet the customer's exact requirements.

Until recently, collecting and managing data to the degree required for customer life cycle analysis was beyond the capability of most organizations. Today, with the availability of eBusiness technology, organizations can easily implement systems to gather information and analyze data in real time, which enables them to continuously refine their understanding of customer behavior, especially as that behavior changes over time. Without this granular level of customer-specific knowledge, organizations cannot develop effective strategies for personalizing the customer experience (Principle Three), optimizing the lifetime value of the customer (Principle Four), or focusing on 100 percent customer satisfaction (Principle Five).

Develop Customer Profiles

Central to every eBusiness strategy is the development of the customer profile, a rich description of key characteristics about each specific customer, including both basic data (demographics, purchasing history, etc.) and information derived from analyzing the customer's life cycle process. The customer profile encodes, for example, observations about which offers appeal most to the customer, which channel(s) the customer prefers, which product attributes the customer values most, how much the customer has spent in the past and is likely to spend in the future, and other issues of strategic relevance. Customer profiles are essential to effective segmentation and predictive modeling.

Segment Customers Based on Relevant Criteria

By analyzing the customer life cycle process, organizations can pinpoint significant differences as well as significant similarities among customers. The job of segmentation is to sort out which differences and similarities are most significant across all customers, and then to divide the customer base into groups based on relevant distinctions. Effective segmentation is greatly aided by the power of eBusiness technology, which enables organizations to capture and analyze large bodies of timely data to discern significant correlations among numerous customer attributes.

In the past, because organizations had no easy way to capture, consolidate, and analyze this data, their segmentation strategies were limited and often based on criteria of little strategic value (such as geography). With eBusiness capabilities, however, organizations are able to segment customers according to far more complex and less obvious factors, such as channel preference, profitability, buying patterns, and other meaningful customer attributes.

Dell, for example, segments its customers into a dozen different groups, based either on the size of the customer or the industry. Speaking at a Forbes CEO Conference in Atlanta, Georgia, in June 1999, Dell founder and CEO Michael Dell commented on his company's segmentation strategy: "We've found that if we segment our business, not only do we get an ability to scale the business faster, but we start to understand the unique needs of specific customers. Instead of creating functional businesses that are really too big to manage and don't integrate very well, we divide and conquer the business. If you go back to 1994, our United States business had a group of large customers. It was a $3.5 billion business. A few years later, we decided to break it up into government and education, mid-size companies and large companies. More recently, we've divided large companies into large companies and global companies to distinguish between their buying criteria. And the government group is now split into federal, state, and local. The education group has been split into K-through-12 and higher education. We now have about twelve of these businesses in the United States, and each one is a $1 billion to $2 billion business."

In the consumer goods industry, companies such as Procter & Gamble, Unilever, and Diageo practice highly sophisticated segmentation strategies by analyzing reams of demographic and purchasing data. This analysis enables these organizations to develop finely detailed "pyschographic" profiles of distinct consumer "types": consumers who purchase Diageo's Johnnie Walker brand of scotch, for instance, will typically fit a pyschographic profile different from that of consumers who purchase its Smirnoff brand of vodka. This sort of analysis is valuable in several ways: it enables consumer-goods manufacturers to more effectively target their advertising and promotion efforts, and it provides insights for the development of new products as well as the refinement of existing brands. But consumer goods organizations face several challenges in conducting this type of segmentation analysis. Because they generally do not sell their products directly to consumers and instead use the retail channel to reach end users, they have limited direct knowledge of their final customers. In addition, the information that they do obtain—from their retail partners, third-party data sources such as Information Resources,

Inc. (a leading provider of consumer purchase data gathered from stores' scanners and from household panels), and their own market research— generally is not available on a real-time (or near real-time) basis. However, the Internet channel now provides consumer-goods producers with a new avenue to communicate directly with consumers about product preferences. Though many consumer-goods companies choose not to sell directly to consumers over the Internet—to avoid causing conflict with their established retail channel partners—many are beginning to use their Web sites to inform customers about their products. Equipped with appropriate eBusiness capabilities to capture the behavior of visitors to their Web sites—what products they were interested in, what information they searched for and how long they spent reviewing it, and so on—these organizations can use this data to learn about their customers and help refine their segmentation strategies.

Avoiding the "Silo Effect"

Many organizations have accumulated enormous amounts of customer information, but because the data are not centralized—and are often scattered across multiple data files in different formats and in disparate, incompatible systems—organizations cannot easily analyze and compare customer data. As a consequence, valuable information is locked away in these "silos." The good news is that by using eBusiness technology, including state-of-the-art technology to integrate these disparate systems, organizations can leverage their existing investments in these data stores without having to start from scratch. At CompUSA, for example, the largest U.S. retailer of desktop computers and software, a version of the silo problem made it difficult for the company's service agents to determine which support services various customers were entitled to. Customer warranty information was stored in back-office systems that were not easily accessible by service agents. When CompUSA came to us, we deployed our Siebel Call Center software to tap into its back-end legacy systems, which included JDA and SAP R/3 applications, enabling agents to resolve customer service issues more quickly. CompUSA's service representatives are now able to view a complete record of the customer—including purchases, past service requests, and service contract status—and deliver the required level of support specified in the warranty. Both sales and service agents at CompUSA's call center use the integrated system, which has resulted in increased sales, a higher rate of problem resolution on the first call, and a decrease in the service dispatch rate.

Predictive Modeling and Customer Profitability

Another key reason for the intensive analysis of customer information is to develop the ability to better predict two things: how much the existing customer is likely to spend in the future (what I identify as Principle Four, "Optimize the lifetime value of the customer," which I'll discuss later in more depth), and which prospects are likely to become profitable customers. The ability to accurately predict the likely profitability of prospects is critical to developing effective strategies and campaigns to acquire new customers. By studying the behavior of existing customers, and how this behavior correlates with various customer attributes, the organization can develop models of which prospects it should target with advertising, promotional offers, and marketing efforts.

Organizations can also use predictive modeling to identify customers who may be likely to defect. For example, our client Rittenhouse Financial Services uses eBusiness software to help predict—with 70 percent accuracy—the likelihood of a customer leaving within three months unless the company intervenes with some recovery action.[5] It does so by analyzing small clusters of customers with similar profiles to identify indicators of potential defection, such as asset transfers and decreased calls. According to the model, a defection from any one cluster means that others within the same cluster are also likely to defect. When the system identifies a potential defector, it then suggests a recovery strategy, and the firm can take specific action to try to keep the customer. In this way, Rittenhouse uses its eBusiness capabilities to discover sources of potential customer dissatisfaction and to anticipate customers' needs, even before customers may be ready to act.

Detailed customer knowledge clearly is the fuel that powers eBusiness success for any organization, regardless of size, industry, or geography. By continuously refining and adding to its store of customer information—and by regularly analyzing that information for deeper insights into customer needs and preferences—an organization enriches and reinforces its bonds with customers. In a world in which competitive advantage now depends on delivering the highest levels of customer satisfaction, the ability to know one's customers in precise detail carries an organization a very long way toward superior competitive performance.

IBM:
Customer-Focused e-Business Enables Integrated Solutions for Customers

If you turn the clock back five years ago, customers purchased different components on their own. A hardware decision was separate from a software decision was separate from a services decision. Today, customers are increasingly looking for a full solution and for a full-service provider. To win in this environment, it is imperative to have an integrated view of your customers.

—DOUG MAINE, GENERAL MANAGER, IBM.COM

IBM AT A GLANCE

Employing more than 300,000 people around the world, IBM finished 2000 with sales of more than $88 billion. The company makes a broad range of computers, including PCs, notebooks, mainframes, and network servers. It also develops software and peripherals, and it derives about 35 percent of sales from its professional-services organization. The company owns Lotus Development, maker of the Lotus Notes messaging system, and Tivoli Systems, which develops tools that manage corporate computer networks. About 60 percent of IBM's sales are to customers outside the United States.

IBM is one of the few technology companies today that can deliver a complete, global solution to its customers, from hardware to software to IT services. Indeed, the breadth of the company's products, services, and operations is nothing short of staggering. Consider these facts:

- Eight of every ten enterprise servers are sold by IBM.
- 70 percent of all corporate data in the world is managed by IBM software.
- IBM holds a 40 percent market share in notebook PC hard drives.
- IBM is the world's largest IT services company.
- IBM Global Financing is the largest financing company in the IT industry.
- IBM operates in 164 countries, has Web sites in more than thirty-one languages, and has more than 90,000 Business Partners globally.

Despite its breadth of capabilities, IBM's practice of going to market with such a wide variety of products and services through numerous semi-autonomous organizational units left the company with a splintered view of its customers, making it more difficult to sell integrated solutions and deliver consistent levels of service. IBM employs a matrix organizational structure whereby its business is organized around six product groups (e.g., Server Group, Software Group) and then further divided along geographic lines (Americas; Europe, Middle East and Africa; and Asia Pacific), customer segments (Enterprise, Global Mid-Market, Global Small), and five specific industry sectors (e.g., Financial Services, Distribution). IBM's sales and marketing organization mirrors this structure, compounding the challenge of maintaining a single view of the customer across the entire enterprise.

Moreover, customers interacting with the company through one or more of its many channels—IBM's face-to-face sales force; IBM Business Partners; and ibm.com, an integrated "TeleWeb" channel of Web sites and call centers—did not always feel that they were working with a single, integrated company intimately in touch with their history, preferences, and needs. "We did not have a complete view of what a given customer was doing across the entire IBM company at a particular point in time," says Doug Maine, General Manager, ibm.com. "We had many stand-alone customer relationship management applications operating inside the company, which inhibited the effectiveness of sales and marketing activities, leading to missed revenue opportunities and lower customer satisfaction."

To address these issues and fully capitalize on the company's ability to deliver total solutions, IBM decided in 1999 to implement a system that would integrate all customer information and customer-facing operations across the enterprise.

Strategic Context of e-Business Implementation

IBM's decision to implement an integrated suite of customer-focused e-business applications falls within the context of the company's larger initiative to transform itself into an e-business. IBM's e-business vision is to Web-enable the entire company, with a specific focus on using the Internet for commerce, procurement, and customer care, as well as for linking processes such as marketing, supply-chain management, and fulfillment. IBM has been promoting its e-business vision since 1995, the year CEO Louis Gerstner made the decision to focus IBM's resources on the Internet. Three global trends supported this decision:

- The exponential growth and use of the Internet by individuals and businesses was beginning to deliver unprecedented access to information and powerful new ways to leverage information.
- The new, global network economy—an intense form of "information capitalism"—was just beginning to thrive, driven by the Net's speed, flexibility, and support of innovation.
- New e-business models began spawning to take advantage of network economics, siphoning customers and profits from traditional businesses.

Committed to leading the emerging network-centric trend, Gerstner shifted 25 percent of IBM's research and development budget into Net projects and declared that every IBM product had to be Internet-friendly. He began to drive software development toward the Java programming language and pushed a crash effort to link Lotus Notes software tightly to the Web. He drove IBM to embrace e-commerce and e-procurement and to Web-enable business processes. And he focused on strengthening IBM's e-business services, such as Web-hosting, to distinguish the company from its competitors.

The results of IBM's transformation to e-business have been impressive. In 2000, IBM sold $23.3 billion worth of products over the Web;

avoided $377 million through the implementation of e-procurement applications with thousands of suppliers; avoided $2 billion in support costs by providing 99 million customer self-service transactions over the Web; and achieved cost-avoidance and productivity gains of over $384 million by delivering 36 percent of its internal training over the Web.

As IBM has made these improvements, however, smaller, more focused competitors have made inroads in some market segments in which IBM competes. While IBM is working diligently to respond to these competitive threats, it has realized that its unique ability to deliver complete solutions is perhaps its most powerful differentiator within today's competitive environment. The "unbundling" of software, hardware, and services has given customers far more choices, but also heightened the need to have someone who can tie all the pieces together—a job for which no company is better qualified than IBM. Yet to capitalize on its unique ability, IBM realized that it needed a comprehensive view of its customers across all of its rapidly growing and diverse lines of business, as well as a comprehensive view of its products and sales opportunities.

IBM also wanted to present itself as an integrated company in order to support its positioning as an exemplar of e-business. "For IBM to persuade customers that they should be running their businesses as e-businesses while not excelling at it ourselves undermines our credibility," says Maine. "We needed a system that would integrate IBM in the eyes of our customers and give customers a 'One IBM' experience."

Creating the Integrated View

To manage the deployment of its customer-focused e-business system, IBM created a global program under the direction of Herb Hunt, Vice President and Business Process Executive for Customer Relationship Management, IBM. The program adopted a phased approach to the implementation in order to maximize the chance of success in each phase by taking advantage of the lessons learned during the prior phases.

The first phase of the implementation focused on IBM's twenty-six worldwide call centers, which support inbound and outbound telesales activities with customers, IBM Business Partners, and IBM employees. Call centers were viewed as the best place to begin the implementation, as they often provide the first customer touch point for gathering, qualifying, and distributing customer information. IBM first deployed its customer-focused e-business applications to call centers in Atlanta, Dallas, Madrid, and Toronto. Call center agents in these locations now have all essential customer and product information at their fingertips. For example, agents can see the entire record of a customer's interactions with IBM, including all purchases and service requests. When handling a service call, this information enables the agent to personalize the conversation, anticipate the customer's needs, and address inquiries promptly and accurately. When engaged in a sales call, the information enables the agent to make better-informed and -targeted recommendations and avoid re-presenting offers that have already been rejected.

As IBM continues deploying its e-business system to the rest of its call centers throughout the world, it has begun the second phase of its deployment by extending this system to its field service and support personnel. Having the call center, field service, and field support personnel on the same system will take IBM an important step closer to having a "closed loop" process for capturing customer information. To further close the customer information loop, IBM will deploy its customer-focused e-business system in subsequent phases to its face-to-face sales force and its Business Partners. Eventually, IBM's call centers will be able to route leads directly to its sales force, and sales personnel will be able to check a customer's record to analyze the customer's transaction history and potential product and service requirements before approaching the account. Service and support personnel will identify sales opportunities in service calls and ensure that the appropriate sales representative from either IBM or an IBM Business Partner contacts these customers.

IBM's partners will be integrated into the company's e-business system via a Web-based partner portal. This portal will enable IBM to manage channel partners as extended virtual sales and service organizations. IBM will manage the opportunities, accounts, and service requests of its channel partners and then track performance on all assigned items. Additionally, IBM's partner portal will enable its channel partners to browse product and pricing information, configure solutions, and generate quotes and online orders, fully automating the partner/vendor relationship.

The company is also in the process of deploying its customer-focused e-business system to its IBM Global Services organization. IBM Global Services, which provides services ranging from consulting to Web page design to hosting online storefronts, will have access to the same consolidated customer information that IBM's call centers and field sales team use. Having this shared view of the customer will enable IBM Global Services to more effectively engage in team selling with the field sales force, because both parties will be fully aware of all sales activities occurring within the account.

To fully close the customer information loop, IBM plans to integrate its marketing operations into its e-business system in 2001. The marketing component of the system will enable IBM to analyze consolidated customer information; align campaigns with appropriate target audiences; plan and execute highly personalized campaigns with the right message at the right time; use preferred communication channels; and measure, monitor, and refine campaign performance to ensure optimal return on investment.

When the deployment of its e-business system is finished in 2001, IBM will have 55,000 employees around the world using a single, integrated system for managing customer relationships. IBM will be positioned to present a single face to its customers and will have a single view of its customers. Through this integration, the company will be able to leverage its full range of capabilities to deliver total solutions to its customers and capture more of their business. "The more you know about each customer's order history, products, services, needs, communication channels, and preferences, the better positioned you are to sell integrated solutions and earn their loyalty," says Maine. "This kind of customer focus puts us on a track to understand, anticipate, and act on customers' needs at the right time and place."

Early Benefits of IBM's
Customer-Focused e-Business System

IBM already knows the value of using information technology to manage customer relationships. The company has been providing dedicated telesales and telecoverage since 1996 to several hundred of its top enterprise customers through its Gold Service program. By providing these large accounts with a consistent point of entry into IBM's breadth of offerings, customers get a "one IBM" experience that integrates face-to-face sales, call center resources, and personalized, one-to-one marketing. The Gold Service program has made IBM an easier company with which to do business, provided IBM with greater reach and coverage, and improved customer satisfaction.

Studies show that Gold Service customized communications and messages reach 89 percent of decision makers, with more than 63 percent recalling the Gold Service mailing because of specific information related to their areas of interest. Customer surveys indicate that more than 90 percent of customers are satisfied with their total Gold Service experience. Additionally, the number of customers who have registered for direct e-mails has jumped by 600 percent, while the actual number of new customer contacts being reached has more than doubled.

Since 1998, IBM has been integrating the Web into the Gold Service program through "e-sites," dedicated extranets between customers and IBM. e-Sites provide information that is personalized to the needs of the Gold Service customer, from contract information to technical information to price lists. Because IBM's e-sites and call centers are integrated, the customer is able to move seamlessly between the two channels to resolve questions, place orders, and submit requests for sales support. In fact, while browsing the Web, Gold Service customers can click on "call me" buttons that trigger immediate phone calls from dedicated IBM call center sales specialists who know the Gold Service customer's history. This system enables IBM's direct sales teams to focus the bulk of their time on selling integrated solutions to customers that address more complex business problems rather than on routine sales and service issues. Furthermore, Maine reports that customers always show a measurable increase in the amount of business they do with IBM once they are put on the Gold Service program. As IBM continues the deployment and optimization of its customer-focused e-business system, the company will offer similar tailored programs for customers of all sizes.

IBM has also seen benefits from integrating its marketing activities with its other sales and support channels. Before integrating its channels, IBM ran print advertisements for new products that informed customers of an offering but did not help the customer move forward in the buying process. Today, IBM's print advertisements direct customers to either an 800 number or a Web page that is specifically linked to the print advertisement. When the customer goes to the Web, he sees content that supplements the print advertisement and is given the option to order the product immediately online. The Web site is synchronized with the 800 number so that the customer can move seamlessly between the Web and call center in seeking answers to questions and placing an order. As Maine says, "We're all about allowing customers to do business with IBM on their own terms." As the customer-focused e-business system extends the linkages between IBM's marketing activities and its sales and support channels, even more benefits are anticipated. For example, in addition to linking marketing campaigns with a specific IBM Web site or 800 number, IBM will be able to link marketing campaigns to the Web sites of its business partners around the world.

Keys to Success

IBM's goal in deploying its customer-focused e-business system is to create a comprehensive view of IBM's customers, across all product lines and geographies, and to provide customers with a single view of IBM. While working to reach that goal, IBM has acquired valuable insights regarding the factors that contribute to the success of such a deployment.

Centralize management—IBM has benefited from having a centralized steering committee to guide the global deployment. The steering committee provides consistent direction, helps define optimal business processes for field sales, Business Partners, ibm.com, service and support, and other customer-facing operations, and ensures that the customer-focused e-business system is configured to support those processes. "Creating a very tight, centralized management team up-front has been a critical success factor," says Gary Burnette, Director, CRM Architecture for IBM. "Members of the team don't all report into the same organization, but they act as a consolidated team and ensure that we avoid developing 'stovepipe' applications for each channel."

"Broad before deep"—IBM has employed a concept the company refers to as "broad before deep" to guide the deployment of its e-business system. The company seeks to implement capabilities that will immediately add value to the business and deploy those capabilities across all customer-facing channels—Web, call center, field sales, field service, partners, and marketing—rather than implementing numerous capabilities in only one channel. This approach will enable IBM to get its e-business system online quickly and to get all customer-facing channels using the system as soon as possible. Once the system is fully operational across all channels, IBM will go back and add capabilities to continually deepen the company's ability to serve its customers.

Minimize customization—IBM has learned the value of using "vanilla software"—that is, not customized—as much as possible. By avoiding the process of customizing software, IBM is able to deploy its e-business system quickly and ensure the ease of future upgrades. One of the methodologies IBM uses to prevent excessive customization is called the "Fit/Gap" methodology. As Burnette explains, "Fit/Gap is a methodology in which we bring end users into a room with a set of business scenarios. We run those business scenarios and we document where the software supports the scenarios and where there are gaps. Then we make a concerted decision about what we're going to do about those gaps. We may choose to wait to resolve the gaps until a later release of the software, or we may decide we have to do some customization. The overall goal is to keep the customization to an absolute minimum so you can deploy more quickly and migrate easily to the next release when it becomes available."

Manage change—IBM has learned that managing change is a critical success factor in an e-business deployment. "By deploying our e-business system, we are changing the way people do their jobs," says Burnette. "We are changing the tools they use, and for some people this is not necessarily a happy experience. As we roll this program forward, we're spending a lot of time communicating and managing expectations, so that people understand what's going to be broken, how long it's going to be broken, and when they can expect the new system to come online." Moreover, IBM realizes the critical importance of ensuring that end users embrace the new system. "You don't get any points if you roll this whole thing out and nobody uses it," explains Burnette. "To address this issue, we're implementing metrics within our e-business system that test the effectiveness of the system and frequency of use among end users. These metrics will enable us to modify our processes, or actually modify the system midstream to address any effectiveness or acceptance issues we're running into."

Looking Forward

IBM has made tremendous strides in transforming itself into an e-business and continues to push aggressively ahead in its effort to provide its customers with complete information technology solutions. For example, LG Investment & Securities Co., Ltd., one of Korea's largest brokerage and underwriting firms, recently turned to IBM to develop and implement a complete, proprietary solution that would enable LG's customers to engage in Web-based trading. "We chose IBM as a strategic partner because of its ability to provide a total solution," explains Soong Suk, senior manager, LG Investment & Securities' information technology planning team. To execute the project, IBM provided the hardware, software, and services, including infrastructure assessment, design, testing, and implementation.

IBM's recent announcement that it will provide an end-to-end desktop solution for Bell Helicopter Textron's U.S. and Canadian operations offers another example of IBM's growing success in selling total solutions. With this installation, IBM will become Bell Helicopter Textron's sole desktop PC provider and will be providing Bell Helicopter Textron with a host of desktop-related services, including helpdesk and deskside support for the 5,500 systems, networking support and maintenance, connectivity, and systems availability. Bell Helicopter Textron will also receive IBM storage subsystems and IBM graphics workstations for its server environment, as well as various IBM options for the desktop, including flat-panel monitors, keyboards, and other hardware components. In addition, Bell Helicopter Textron will install IBM's Tivoli software to help manage the company's desktop environment, and IBM Global Financing will finance the transaction.

With its customer-focused e-business system coming online, selling these integrated solutions will become increasingly efficient, because all IBM personnel and IBM business partners involved in a project will share a single view of the customer's history, business requirements, and preferences. "Our e-business system plays a pivotal role in our strategy to provide complete solutions to our customers," concludes Maine. "The implementation of the system will enable IBM to work more aggressively with our customers than ever before, anticipate their needs, and provide the industry's highest levels of customer satisfaction across all of our lines of business and channels."

CHAPTER TEN

Principle Two: Use Multiple Channels to Interact with Customers

In the era of eBusiness, no single trend affects organizations more than the expansion of both distribution and communications channels. Certainly the Internet has contributed enormously to this trend: virtually no major organization can survive today without enabling its customers to conduct business or communicate with it via the Web and e-mail. But even before the advent of the Internet, many organizations faced increasing pressure to accommodate customers through a broader range of channels. During the 1980s and 1990s, for example—following deregulation of the phone industry and the resulting decline in rates for toll-free service—organizations across all sectors added call centers to their channel mix at a rapid pace. This trend profoundly affected many industries, including direct order businesses such as Lands' End and L.L. Bean; in the past, these catalog companies took their orders exclusively through the mail, but most of their orders now come through the call center, and an increasing number come in over the Web.

This expansion of channels poses a highly complex problem for organizations: how to synchronize interactions with prospects and customers over time and across all channels, without dropping the connection. That is to say, customers do not limit themselves to a single channel. Rather, they randomly traverse channels, choosing the channel that is most convenient or effective for the situation at hand. But at the same time, the customer assumes that the organization will recognize him every step of the way: the customer expects the next channel to pick up the line of communication where it left off.

This multichannel coordination problem can be solved only by implementing a global eBusiness architecture that enables the organization to track and record, in real time, every customer interaction at every touch point. The rewards of this multichannel capability are considerable. For example, a well-coordinated use of multiple channels can dramatically improve an organization's sales efficiency. Research indicates that a multichannel strategy can reduce selling costs by 20 to 50 percent.[6] Such reductions are achieved, for example, by using low-cost, low-touch channels to develop and qualify sales leads, then switching to a higher cost, high-touch channel (such as the direct sales force) to close the sale.

But the benefits of a multichannel strategy extend far beyond reduced selling costs. A multichannel strategy enables organizations to reach more potential customers. In most markets, any one channel accounts for no more than 50 percent of the potential market volume, and in many markets that proportion is far less than half.[7] Therefore, in order to thoroughly cover a market and be in position to compete for a significant share of the market, an organization will need to employ several channels.

Even more, offering customers multiple channels can produce channel synergy—that is, the effect of the channels working together is more than just the sum of the benefits of each individual channel. Compelling evidence of the synergistic effect of a multichannel strategy is found in the retail brokerage industry. In the last few years, with the rise of numerous Internet brokers such as Datek, e-Trade, and Ameritrade, competition for the individual investor's brokerage business has become brutal. Yet despite the onslaught of these pure online firms—who boast deep discount commissions—the clear winner in this ferocious marketplace has been the established stalwart, Charles Schwab & Co., whose commissions are generally higher than those of the online discounters.

According to a study by the consulting firm McKinsey & Company, Schwab has far outpaced the pack: Schwab, a customer of ours since 1995, has managed to spend far less in advertising and marketing per new customer than any of its online competitors, while simultaneously achieving higher average assets per customer account.[8] In other words, Schwab is able to attract a higher-quality customer than can its competitors, at a lower cost. McKinsey concluded that a major reason for Schwab's remarkable success is its multichannel strategy: unlike its Internet-only competitors, Schwab interacts with its customers through multiple channels—branch offices, telephone, and the Internet. A McKinsey study of the retail industry provided additional confirming evidence: the consulting firm found that customers of organizations with multiple channels—Internet, stores, and catalog—spend on average more than four times as much as customers of Internet-only firms.

Anecdotal evidence from various multichannel organizations confirms McKinsey's findings. Williams-Sonoma, for example, sells specialty items through the Web, catalogs, and more than 300 stores. Cathy Halligan, Williams-Sonoma vice president of marketing, told *Direct Marketing* magazine that "customers who have at least one catalog-only item in his or her order history spend significantly more at retail than those customers with no catalog-only purchases."[9] Lands' End, a retailer of apparel and other personal products that started out in 1963 as a mail-order company, takes orders both over the phone and on the Web. In 1999, it sent out 250 million catalogs to its customers, and received about 10 percent of its orders online. Just as phone orders spike right after catalogs arrive at customers' homes, so do its Internet orders. "We thought going into E-commerce it would be a different business," an Internet analyst at Lands' End told *The New Yorker* magazine. "But it's the same business, the same patterns, the same contacts. It's an extension of what we already do."[10] For Dell Computer, the Internet appears to have a synergistic effect on the call center: Dell recently discovered that half of its customers who ordered its products over the telephone had first visited the company's Web site.

The McKinsey findings point to a correlation between higher-value customers and multichannel strategy. What accounts for this correlation? A large part of the answer is that some customer segments significantly value having a choice of channels by which to interact with a vendor—and multichannel organizations appeal to those segments. To return to Schwab, for example, some 70 percent of new customer accounts come into Schwab via its 360 branch offices, but customers make nearly 90 percent of their trades over the Internet. At the same time, the company's call center handles more than 10 million customer calls per month. Indeed, some 95 percent of Schwab customers use all channels to interact with the company. Schwab customers clearly prefer a choice of channels: they use them all, and are willing to pay a premium for having the choice.

The benefits of a multichannel strategy appear inarguable based on such measurable results. Clearly, a handful of early adopters have distanced themselves from their competitors by the well-coordinated use of multiple channels, supported by comprehensive, customer-focused information systems. Now the message appears to be getting out: organizations of every type and every size have begun to perceive the powerful benefits of a multichannel strategy and are actively endeavoring to construct their own multichannel strategies. In retail, for example, companies as diverse as Eddie Bauer and Office Depot are incorporating the Internet, catalogs, and stores into their go-to-market strategies. The question remains, however, how effectively these and other organizations will integrate and execute their use of multiple channels. The point is not simply to conduct business through multiple channels but to synchronize channels so that customers can enjoy seamless interactions with the organization no matter which channel the customer uses at any given moment. In devising their multichannel strategies, organizations must keep in mind several key guidelines.

Identify Customer Channel Preferences

While customers use multiple channels if given the choice, they will tend to use them in fairly consistent ways. For example, some banking customers may regularly use teller service to make deposits and ATMs to make withdrawals, while others exclusively use one or the other for both deposits and withdrawals. It is important, therefore, to identify these sorts of channel preferences, and to structure channel capabilities and balance them accordingly. Moreover, in order to ensure that customers' usage of different channels is economically optimal for the organization, it must create processes and incentives that direct customers to the most cost-effective channel for a specific type of interaction. To return to banking, for example, some banks impose a surcharge for conducting certain transactions through a teller rather than an ATM. In this regard, nearly every organization could benefit enormously by providing self-service capabilities to customers over the Web, and over the telephone using interactive voice recognition (IVR) technology.

Indeed, extending self-service capabilities to customers is a powerful way to increase both customer satisfaction and employee productivity. For example, Honeywell's Industrial Control business unit—a provider of advanced control software and industrial automation systems, with $2.5 billion in sales—faced the challenge of reducing the time required to resolve customers' service requests. Headquartered in Phoenix, over the years the unit had built a database of solutions to many types of problems that occur in manufacturing plants. However, this information was for internal use only—customers could not access it directly to resolve problems themselves.

To rectify this problem, Honeywell implemented a Web-based self-service system that consolidates solutions to more than 50,000 problems in a common database and makes those solutions available to customers and Honeywell field technicians worldwide. "Our goal is to never discover a problem twice," says Rob Baxter, VP and CIO, Honeywell Industrial Control. "Once we've discovered a problem, we communicate it to everyone in the support chain so they are aware of it." Customers are now able to resolve many common problems on their own and field technicians can be more efficient. International customers have found the self-service system especially valuable. As Baxter explains, "If a customer has a problem in Singapore, they need to be able to get the right information as quickly as possible without having to go through a whole series of people that they may not know."

Honeywell now has customers and field engineers in more than sixty countries using its online service application. If customers are not able to resolve a problem on their own using the site's knowledge base, they can submit or update service requests on the site and add attachments to a service request that further explain the problem. In addition, the application allows customers to fill out a customer feedback survey for each survey request, helping Honeywell ensure complete customer satisfaction. According to Baxter, Honeywell's "customer delight" is now an industry-leading 98.1 percent.

Organizations also need to ensure that they are communicating with customers through the customers' preferred communications channel. Some customers, for example, do not respond well to telemarketing campaigns, regardless of when they are called or the nature of the offer. However, those same customers may respond very positively to the exact same offer if it is communicated to them by e-mail. It is critical, therefore, that organizations track customers' channel preferences, because employing the wrong channel can lead to disaster. One powerful benefit of an eBusiness approach to the design and execution of marketing campaigns is the ability to rapidly and precisely test the effects of different channels (as well as different offers, segments, and so on). Using eMarketing software, for instance, an organization can divide the targeted customer or prospect list into any number of test cells and track the results of each cell by channel (among other numerous variables that could also be tracked). One test cell might deliver the offer via direct mail, a second via a phone call, and a third via an e-mail containing a link to a page on the organization's Web site. By managing the entire campaign through the eBusiness system, which encodes every offer so that the results can be specifically tied to the individual test cells, the organization can determine which channel produces the greatest response, and at what cost. The organization can then microanalyze the results to determine, for instance, which types of customers responded to which channel, offer, etc. The organization can then use this information to adjust the rollout of the campaign.

Synchronize Channels So That Customers Have Continuous, Seamless Experience

Whether the customer interacts with the organization by e-mail, letter, fax, in person, or over the phone, the organization must record and track these interactions over time and across all touch points in order to maintain this ongoing dialogue. This is critical to achieving total customer satisfaction. If, for example, a customer sends an e-mail to the organization complaining about a recent experience, then follows up with a

phone call the next day, the customer expects that the service representative will be aware of the earlier e-mail. Yet few organizations have synchronized channels to this extent.

By contrast, in a fully implemented eBusiness system, the customer's
e-mail complaint in the above example would enter a "universal queue"
in the organization's customer care center, where agents are able to
respond to service inquiries that come in via any channel (e-mail, telephone, the Web, fax, etc.). Every inquiry that comes in goes into this single queue, which applies specific rules to govern the routing of each
inquiry, its urgency, and so on. In the case of the e-mail complaint, an
effective eBusiness application would automatically analyze the e-mail,
searching its contents for information to determine to which agent the
e-mail should be routed, and checking the customer's e-mail address
against the customer database to precisely identify the customer and to
determine, for instance, the customer's status (high value, low value).
Within several minutes, the software sends an e-mail reply to the customer, indicating that a service representative will be following up soon.
In this case, suppose that the eBusiness system has determined that the
e-mail has come from a long-term frequent buyer. With our software,
the e-mail gets escalated to high priority and immediately gets routed to
an agent specially trained to deal with that type of complaint. The agent
has a complete view of the customer's information on a screen in front
of him, including purchasing history. The agent also has immediate
access to a comprehensive knowledge base of product and support information. Now, instead of the customer making the follow-up call, the
agent proactively telephones the customer within minutes and is able to
solve the customer's problem in a single call—with no need to have the
customer provide personal information, which is already in the system,
and no need to have the customer repeat the content of the e-mail.
Organizations thus able to coordinate multichannel interactions have a
powerful tool for satisfying and delighting customers.

Understand the Cost Structure of Each Channel

Whether using the channel for marketing, sales, or service, the underlying concept of channel optimization is to balance the cost of the channel

against other factors, including value to the customer, the customer's preferences, and (in a selling situation) the profit potential. Consider, for example, the range of channel costs for a typical bank:

- teller transaction: $1.00
- call center transaction: $.50
- ATM transaction: $.25
- Web transaction: $.01

Clearly, the bank will want to direct as many transactions as possible to the Web. But this channel is not suitable for every transaction (a cash withdrawal, for example), and some customers prefer not to conduct transactions over the Web at all.

Optimize Channel Strategy by Mapping Products and Customers to Appropriate Channels, Based on Cost/Benefit Analysis

An organization's use of multiple channels must be guided by cost/benefit analysis to ensure that it is gaining optimal returns from its multichannel strategy. In many industries, organizations must employ, for example, a combination of field sales representatives working in conjunction with third parties (partners and resellers) in order to deliver a complete solution to customers. Microsoft, for example, deploys a direct sales force that works with its global reseller partners, who fulfill and service Microsoft applications. At the same time, Microsoft augments resellers' activities through its own customer service call centers and via self-service facilities available on Microsoft Web sites. Given the high cost of maintaining a direct sales force—an estimated $500 per customer call (compared to an estimated $5 per telemarketing call)—use of the field sales channel must be limited to large-volume, high-margin accounts that justify the cost. These economics are driving many organizations to add lower-cost channels, including call centers, e-mail, and the Web.

But lower cost is not the only motivation driving organizations to expand channels. Several years ago, for instance, PC maker Gateway concluded that its combination of Web and call center channels could not reach consumers who prefer to see and touch a computer before they buy, a segment that by some estimates accounts for as much as 50 percent of all PC shoppers. Gateway had to assess the costs of developing a channel that could tap this market segment—one that Dell had decided it would not serve—versus the potential benefits from doing so. In the end, the company decided to commit several hundred million dollars to launch its chain of Gateway Country Stores, which now total nearly 300. Rather than carry inventory, however, the stores serve as demonstration showrooms for its products. Customers can come in to try out any model, then place an order at the store, over the Web, or via the call center. Gateway builds the machine to order and ships it to the customer. Thus, Gateway's cost/benefit calculus determined that the retail channel would yield a positive return, but only if the model was structured to avoid incurring excessive inventory costs.

Cost/benefit analysis clearly indicates that the Web offers a tremendously cost-effective sales, service, and marketing channel. However, organizations should not assume that migrating customer activity to the Web will necessarily reduce activity in other channels. Consider, for example, the experience of IBM's sales operations. "Many people think the Web is going to replace the call center, but because the Web is so pervasive, we're getting 30 percent more calls," Fred Fassman, IBM's VP for Global Call Centers, told *Selling Power* magazine. "The Web will replace the more mundane call center functions like providing information, but if the product is complicated, the customer still wants to speak to somebody later in the sales cycle. So we're getting more calls from better-educated customers who want to know the finer points of selecting one software package over another."[11]

Indeed, organizations will likely experience more of this cross-channel interaction, with one channel driving activity in another channel. At Lands' End, for example, Web customers can use a feature called "Lands' End Live" to connect with a live customer service agent. By clicking a button, customers can choose to interact by phone (the agent calls the customer) or through a real-time chat session. This gives customers both the control and rich content of the online experience along with the immediacy of the live interaction. One effect of this feature is that it invites online shoppers to make use of the live-agent resource, which adds some cost to the online channel. But given that fewer than 2 percent of visitors to online shopping sites actually make a purchase, organizations may find that the extension of live agents into the online channel can significantly improve that ratio.

This blended approach to customer care, which combines the Internet and the call center, is especially valuable in the sale and support of complex products and services, and can significantly improve the quality of the customer experience. In these situations, the customer will perform much of the basic information gathering or product/service configuration online without assistance. When the customer has exhausted his own abilities, he clicks on a "Call Me Now" button, which instantaneously sends a request that a live agent call the customer immediately. When the representative calls—either directly over the Internet (using "voice over IP" technology) or via a second phone line—the eBusiness system already has recorded all the information from the customer's online session. Therefore, the representative, now up to date on the customer's current status and needs, can provide added value without requiring the customer to repeat information or backtrack steps on the Web. By using online-collaboration capabilities, such as those available in our Siebel eCollaboration software, the live agent can view the same Web page that the customer is viewing and can assist him or her, for example, in filling out a form or in configuring a product or service in real time.

One trend now sweeping through the "New Economy" and certain to continue is the use of non–Internet channels by an increasing number of dot-com companies. The recent experience of online postage provider Stamps.com provides a good example of this phenomenon at work. Upon going live in late 1999, Stamps.com faced considerable challenges in providing support to customers via the Internet. The response to the company's new product and service offerings was overwhelming. As a consequence, Stamps.com did not anticipate the sheer number and variety of customer service inquiries it would receive. Customer satisfaction was in jeopardy. Almost instantly, Stamps.com had to add call center capabilities. The company came to us for help. By implementing Siebel Call Center, Stamps.com was able to start tracking customers and calls within a few weeks. Ultimately, the company added other eBusiness applications, including sales force automation capabilities and the ability to interface with the Web site and the data warehouse. Their new system also gives managers expanded reporting and statistical analysis tools, enabling them to track various customer metrics and gather information from other business applications. According to Richard Stables, Director of Application Development at Stamps.com, the system has "provided huge cost savings," as well as a single interface to company data across the enterprise. As a result, Stamps.com is able to understand and serve its customers more effectively.

Threadneedle Investment Services: Investing in Customer Satisfaction

Our customer-focused eBusiness system will become the core of all of our business processes.

—PHIL GOFFIN, HEAD OF eBUSINESS,
THREADNEEDLE INVESTMENT SERVICES

THREADNEEDLE AT A GLANCE

Established in 1994 and based in London, Threadneedle Investment Services Ltd. offers mutual funds and other asset-management services to retail and institutional clients. Doing 95 percent of its business through financial intermediaries—independent financial advisers, brokers, banks—the company has quickly risen to become the third-largest retail fund manager in the United Kingdom, and the fourth-largest in Germany. With more than $70 billion in funds under management and more than 1,000 employees, Threadneedle is quickly becoming a fund-management leader throughout Europe. The company is part of the Zurich Financial Services Group, which provides a wide array of insurance and asset-management services on a global basis.

As a relatively new entrant in Europe's fund-management marketplace, Threadneedle Investment Services Ltd. has enjoyed great success in selling its mutual funds and other asset-management services. In less than six years, Threadneedle has become the third-largest retail fund manager in the United Kingdom and one of the largest retail foreign investment companies in Germany. Although fund performance has been the cornerstone of this success, the company believes that its constant focus on improving its "service proposition" has played a pivotal role in driving its exemplary business growth. "Obviously, fund performance is a significant decision criteria for a client," says Phil Goffin, Threadneedle's Head of eBusiness. "But if two funds provide similar results, the choice may well boil down to which company is easier to do business with." To provide its clients with the highest standards of service, the company has placed a great deal of emphasis on developing a multichannel eBusiness system. Threadneedle presents an excellent example of how a company can build such a system incrementally—first, by using eBusiness applications to address a specific business problem, and then extending the eBusiness platform to all customer-facing channels.

Threadneedle's Origins

The British American Tobacco (BAT) group established Threadneedle in 1994 by merging the asset-management businesses of two of its subsidiaries, Allied Dunbar and Eagle Star (both providers of investments and various forms of insurance). Zurich Financial Services (ZFS) acquired the financial services arm of BAT, and hence Threadneedle, in 1998 to create a single, more powerful asset-management company that could capitalize on the growing interest in equity investments among European investors.

Having established a successful investment record with institutional investors during its first three years as an entity, Threadneedle established a retail division in 1997. Today, the retail division accounts for approximately 20 percent of Threadneedle's business. Ninety-five percent of the retail division's business is generated by financial intermediaries—such as independent financial advisers, banks, or brokers—who sell Threadneedle funds to retail investors for a fee, or load. After an intermediary places an order for a Threadneedle fund (on behalf of a retail investor), either the intermediary or the retail investor may contact Threadneedle regarding fund valuations, additional purchases, the switching or selling of shares, or other inquiries. Threadneedle's retail division sells to intermediaries in the United Kingdom and Europe with a broker sales force of eighteen individuals—twelve in the United Kingdom and six in Europe. In the United Kingdom, Threadneedle's retail division also sells through Allied Dunbar's sales force of over 5,000 individuals. The Allied Dunbar sales force accounts for approximately 20 percent of Threadneedle's U.K. sales.

Threadneedle was the first company in Europe to convert an entire range of unit trusts into an umbrella Open-Ended Investment Company (OEIC). OEICs sell mutual funds, often consisting of equity investments, to the public. The term arises from the fact that the firm continually creates new shares on demand. Mutual fund shareholders buy the shares at net asset value and can redeem them at any time at the prevailing market price.

By pioneering OEICs in Europe, Threadneedle attracted tremendous investor interest. European investors—especially German investors—had become unsatisfied with the conservative returns offered by government bonds and were eager to invest in equity mutual funds. "Investors throughout Europe were beginning to wake up to equity funds," says David Carter, Systems Architect for Threadneedle. "They realized that government bonds alone are not going to provide a foundation for a strong income when you retire."

Increased Business Volume Strains Internal Processes

The tremendous growth in demand for Threadneedle funds taxed the company's business processes and provided the first impetus to develop an eBusiness system. In particular, Threadneedle's "dealing process"—that is, the process by which it moved an order through its client service and registration system, often called a "transfer agency system"—required reengineering. The dealing process was paper-based and involved a series of separate, manual steps. First, retail investors would receive an application for a Threadneedle fund from a financial intermediary, fill it out, attach a check or send a separate bank payment, and then either mail it to Threadneedle directly or have the financial intermediary mail it to Threadneedle. Once in Threadneedle's hands, the application had to be "validated"—all aspects of the application had to be reviewed for accuracy, the investor's check had to be verified or the bank payment matched to the application form, and the investment needed to be priced. Then the investment had to be entered into one of Threadneedle's two transfer agency systems, running on two separate computer systems: one for the U.K. business and one for the European business. If an application was incomplete, Threadneedle would send a letter to the retail investor, keeping track of all correspondence using a spreadsheet. "It was a very paper-based, labor-intensive business process," says Carter. "You can only throw so many people at an inherently laborious process—eventually you need to change the process itself."

In addition to having an inefficient dealing process, Threadneedle's call center was hard-pressed to handle a steadily increasing number of calls, usually from retail investors wanting to know the current value of their holdings. There are on average now 8,000 calls per month. "When Threadneedle launched its retail business, we quickly put in a call center with a homegrown application," explains Carter. "It was an effective Visual Basic application with a customer database. However, it supported only the U.K. business and not Europe. Also installed was a telephony switch to manage call queuing, and that was about it. We always knew that as volumes increased, we would have to introduce better servicing systems."

To improve its dealing process and its ability to handle increased call volume, Threadneedle began investigating eBusiness solutions in late 1998. Goffin says the discussion about which eBusiness applications to purchase initiated a more strategic discussion about how to address the larger opportunities and threats facing the company. "We really weren't thinking about eBusiness at first, because we didn't have the systems in place that could support something like that," he says. "But when we began to think strategically about how technology would change the industry, we realized that addressing the issues in our call center and dealing process could be the stepping-stone to an eBusiness transformation. We could use eBusiness software to integrate our business processes and channels to deliver a superior service proposition."

Need for Multichannel eBusiness Solution

At the time that Threadneedle was first exploring eBusiness applications, its marketing, sales, and service groups did not operate in an integrated system—each group handled their duties separately and could not easily access customer information from the others. "We didn't have a 360-degree view of our clients," says Goffin. "For example, we were unable to see what impact our marketing activities were having on sales. Also, information gathered by our field sales force had to be manually synchronized with the information in our call center system in Swindon, England, so we had difficulty maintaining a single view of our interactions with our customers."

Also driving Threadneedle to consider a multichannel eBusiness system was the trend toward using electronically based channels in the fund-management marketplace. As use of the Internet proliferated, financial intermediaries began to seek ways to work more efficiently via the Web. For example, financial intermediaries wanted to buy and sell funds from fund-management companies through electronic message exchanges. An electronic message exchange enables intermediaries to link their retail client back-office systems directly to a fund-management company's product system in order to reduce costs and improve the speed with which they can buy and sell units and obtain valuations on behalf of their clients. In addition, instead of having to complete and post multiple application forms to purchase funds from a combination of management companies, an electronic message exchange enables intermediaries to complete a single application online and send it directly to select fund-management companies over the Internet.

Another electronic channel that had become increasingly important is the "fund supermarket," where financial intermediaries (and retail investors) could "shop" at one Web site for funds from a variety of fund-management companies. A fund supermarket differs from an electronic message exchange in that a fund supermarket is typically a full administration service and system, whereas an electronic message exchange is a neutral electronic data exchange network. The "owner" of a fund supermarket (e.g., Fidelity Investments) offers a combination of investment products and aggregated portfolio-management services. The owner of the fund supermarket charges a small management fee to other financial institutions to list products on the site and charges retail investors for managing their portfolio.

Regarding the development of both fund supermarkets and electronic order processing, Goffin says, "It was apparent that technology was beginning to drive significant change in our industry by providing a variety of new ways to serve the customer. We came to realize that if we weren't able to manage new channels in an integrated fashion, we wouldn't be able to see the whole picture of who is buying what. That, in turn, would prevent us from providing the best possible service and optimizing our sales." In other words, Threadneedle needed eBusiness technology that would allow it to link its business processes to new electronic channels and support new initiatives that would help strengthen the position of its core customers—the intermediaries—in the fund-management marketplace. Threadneedle management thus decided to move forward with the implementation of a comprehensive eBusiness solution. "By thinking big and envisioning how one eBusiness platform could serve as the core of all our business processes, all of the pieces started coming together," says Goffin. "The challenge was developing a system that could bring together our internal processes, the Internet, and all of our other electronic and non-electronic channels to create an efficient system of doing business and better serving the intermediaries."

First Stages of Implementing a Comprehensive eBusiness System

Having developed its eBusiness vision, Threadneedle focused the first stage of its eBusiness implementation on addressing the shortcomings of its dealing process and call center. "Simply getting business on the books and handling inquiries to our call center were our greatest points of pain in the beginning," says Carter. "We felt that we had to address those issues first, and then we could extend our eBusiness platform to improve how we secured business and provided service to our customers through our field sales force and other channels."

The first eBusiness applications deployed by Threadneedle enabled the company to scan paper application forms and other correspondence from customers into a digital file image management system and consolidate those files with the rest of a customer's electronic profile.

The eBusiness applications enabled anyone within Threadneedle's 200-person call center in Swindon, England, to view a customer's entire record through a Web-based interface. "We were immediately able to improve our ability to track all the fragments of information required to open an account and place an order," says Carter. "Our call center agents had complete visibility of a customer's application and all other correspondence. Our eBusiness software provided a digital dashboard for entering and tracking orders, providing valuations, and addressing inquiries. The applications' workflow feature also allowed us to automatically route service requests to customer service teams within Threadneedle that specialize in handling certain customer requests, such as requests for literature, valuation reports, and so forth."

Extending the eBusiness System

After deploying eBusiness applications in its call center, Threadneedle began to extend its eBusiness deployment to additional channels. It started by integrating the eBusiness applications in its call center with a recently formed electronic message exchange in the United Kingdom called EMX. Threadneedle had helped create EMX with a group of other fund-management companies in the United Kingdom to help address customers' increasing desire to conduct business electronically. By integrating its eBusiness system with EMX, Threadneedle gained the ability to automatically validate an order placed through EMX, process the order, and consolidate the order with the rest of a customer's record. Having this consolidated record allows Threadneedle to easily review valuations if they are contested at a later date and ensure seamless service if an intermediary should decide to contact Threadneedle's call center about an order placed through EMX. "In many cases, an intermediary will request a valuation through EMX and then contact our call center thirty minutes later to check the information—or worse, the intermediary could call three days later to check the information or use the information for dealing," says Carter. "We're able to store records of all interactions with the customer—whether they take place through EMX or over the phone—in XML format in our common customer database so we can easily resolve questions or disputes." XML (Extensible Markup Language) enables Threadneedle to translate electronic data received via EMX (and other electronic channels) into a common "Threadneedle language" that is then used to populate a customer's comprehensive record.

Having integrated its eBusiness system with EMX, Threadneedle is now focused on launching a fund supermarket with three other fund-management companies (Gartmore, Jupiter, and M&G). The distinguishing feature of this new fund supermarket, called "Cofunds," is that it is exclusively for financial intermediaries—it will have no direct retail business. Cofunds' goal is to provide a consolidated solution for the administration of "open architecture" investment products. These products enable intermediaries to combine the best funds from many product providers into a single end-investor product, as well as make it easy to switch across product providers in the future. The launch of Cofunds is intended to help Threadneedle further strengthen its relationship with financial intermediaries.

"In the United States, the fund supermarkets are dominated by two major players, Fidelity Investments and Charles Schwab," explains Carter. "From Threadneedle's standpoint, the best way to support the relationship that exists between financial intermediaries and their customers (retail investors) was to create an independent fund supermarket geared entirely toward helping the financial intermediaries better serve their customers. Cofunds is taking a lead from Threadneedle and it will implement a derivative of the eBusiness system supporting Threadneedle to handle and support the relationships between product providers and intermediaries that work through Cofunds. Cofunds is engaged in an active campaign to bring other fund-management companies into the supermarket to expand the product offerings available to the intermediaries. By doing business with Cofunds, the intermediaries will be able to maintain their relationship with their customers and we will be able to maintain our relationship with the intermediaries, which is different from the general supermarket model which disintermediates these relationships."

When intermediaries place an order for a Threadneedle fund at the Cofunds site, the information about that order, including information on the intermediary, will be automatically made available to Threadneedle's eBusiness system, thereby ensuring that Threadneedle maintains a complete record of its interactions with the intermediary regardless of how he interacts with Threadneedle. "Our sales executives will be able to see which brokers have been buying which funds, and through which channel—Cofunds, EMX, or direct," says Carter. "This visibility will allow our salespeople to strengthen their relationship with the intermediaries, because they will better understand what the intermediaries are interested in and how they are processing their business with Threadneedle."

To achieve a closed loop of customer information between Cofunds and the sales team, Threadneedle will be deploying its eBusiness system to its sales team at the same time it launches Cofunds. Currently, the personnel in Threadneedle's sales force use a variety of contact management systems, none of which is integrated with the Swindon-based call center. As a result, when a field salesman visits an intermediary, the salesman has no way of seeing the intermediary's recent interactions with Threadneedle via the Threadneedle call center or EMX. This lack of visibility hinders the salesperson's ability to suggest new Threadneedle funds that are aligned with the intermediary's purchasing patterns and hinders his ability to provide the intermediary with a seamless service experience. "By extending our eBusiness system to our field sales force, we will be able to create an uninterrupted dialogue between Threadneedle and the intermediaries regardless of how they choose to interact with us," says Carter. "We will also be able to increase the speed with which we can put new business on the books. When a salesman goes to visit a new broker in Germany, for example, he will be able to capture much of the basic information required to register the prospect, and then electronically send that information directly to our Client Services division in order for them to process the new business. Ultimately, this will accelerate the dealing process, enable the call center representatives to keep track of any special arrangements made with the intermediary [i.e., a special commission rate], and allow our sales managers to keep better track of deal volumes, commissions, and so forth."

Before the end of 2001, Threadneedle also plans to tighten the integration between its eBusiness system and its Web site. Currently,

Threadneedle's Web site is a "stand-alone" site that is not integrated with Threadneedle's call center or any of its other channels. Moreover, the Web site is used primarily as a means of delivering marketing messages to intermediaries; it is not possible to get valuations or place new orders via the Threadneedle Web site. By integrating the Threadneedle Web site with the company's other channels and increasing the Web site's functionality, Threadneedle hopes to further differentiate itself in the European fund-management marketplace. "Currently, there are a lot of loose ends between the marketing department, call center, sales force, and our customers, so we don't actually know very well who is using our Web site," says Carter. "By extending our eBusiness system to our Web site, we will be able to consolidate Web-based interactions with the rest of the customer's record, so when the customer contacts our call center after visiting the Web site, the call center rep will be able to ask the customer questions such as, 'What did you think of the Web site, how can we make it more useful, did you find everything you were looking for, etc.' It would allow us to turn routine call center interactions into much more productive discussions for both the customer and Threadneedle."

As another step in tightening the integration between its Web site and its eBusiness platform, Threadneedle is planning to allow intermediaries to execute transactions directly on its Web site. "We would like to provide trusted intermediaries with access over the Web to the very same 'digital dashboard' we have in our call center so that the intermediary could actually process a deal themselves," says Carter. "Furthermore, for all intermediaries, we would like to provide a deal-tracking system on our Web site much like the FedEx package tracking system, whereby an intermediary can see exactly where a deal stands. This visibility could become quite important to an intermediary, bearing in mind that he doesn't get his commission until the deal has been completed." Carter adds that Threadneedle will soon introduce functionality on its site that will allow both intermediaries and retail investors to get fund valuations over the Web. Currently, more than 40 percent of calls to the Threadneedle call center are for simple valuations. Shifting these basic calls to the Web self-service channel will free call center staff to focus on more complex service requests.

Threadneedle's Future State

When its eBusiness system is fully deployed, Threadneedle will have a closed-loop customer information system that will consolidate all interactions with customers in a common database, regardless of whether the interactions take place through the call center, EMX, the field sales force, Cofunds, or Threadneedle's Web site. "We will be able to offer intermediaries a level of support that is unrivaled in our market," says Goffin. "Our employees will have the tools to access a full view of the client at all times. By integrating the information we obtain from different sources and channels, we will ensure that deals and valuations are processed faster and that we are providing our clients with the most up-to-date and accurate information. Moreover, we will be able to see a 360-degree view of each client so that our sales and service processes seamlessly work together.

"As the market expands and we continue our rapid growth, we believe that Threadneedle is well positioned to integrate with Zurich Financial Services and expand our reach through electronic and non-electronic channels," concludes Goffin. "Our eBusiness platform is enabling us to become a more unified, nimble company that is able to adapt to any market changes, and provide the best service in the European fund-management industry."

CHAPTER ELEVEN

Principle Three: Personalize the Customer Experience

Before the advent of mass communication and mass marketing, nearly all business was conducted in local markets—or face-to-face by sales and service professionals—with direct interaction between buyer and seller. There was a high degree of personalization in the relationship between merchants and their customers: merchants knew customers by name, made note of their preferences and pocketbooks, and acted as trusted advisers to their best customers. However, as organizations grew larger and larger—exploiting the advantages of scale from mass production and distribution—they also often grew more distant from their customers: the one-to-one intimacy that once characterized the customer relationship all but disappeared.

Today's eBusiness technologies enable organizations to reinfuse their customer relationships with one-to-one personalization. They enable organizations to return to relationship-based marketing, sales, and service—and thereby reap the benefits of improved customer loyalty.

Why do customers care about a personalized experience? In other words, why should organizations care? There are several reasons. Most individuals appreciate the sense of being recognized as a unique customer, and feel ensured that their specific needs are being addressed. But the primary reason is that well-implemented personalization makes it easier, more efficient, and more pleasant for customers to interact with an organization. Personalization means that the customer's individual preferences are taken into consideration. In the era of eBusiness, personalization is not, for example, simply placing the customer's name in the salutation of a direct-mail piece ("Dear Mr. Smith . . ."). It means, instead, that the customer receiving that mailing was selected because the organization knows something relevant about Mr. Smith that indicates that he is highly likely to be interested in the content of that mailing. It would be a waste of both his time and the organization's resources to send a mailing that did not interest him. Using eBusiness technology, organizations can continuously fine-tune their knowledge about customers and prospects, so that they can better target customers who most value their offerings. This ability to match the value of the offering to the customer's preferences is the essence of personalization.

Personalization is a powerful tool for developing loyalty. Two of the leading Web search sites, Yahoo! and Excite, for example, both enable their visitors to personalize various features of their sites—including news, weather, stock portfolio, and so on. Both have discovered that visitors who use these personalization features return to the site five times more often than users who do not take advantage of those features.

In a business-to-business context, personalization enables organizations to tailor offerings, content, services, and processes based on a customer's status, preferences, and other attributes. For example, Chicago-based FMC FoodTech, a leading vendor of food-processing systems to customers ranging from Tyson Foods to independent produce suppliers, is implementing software to create a single ordering channel through the Web. Customers will have a personal Web page listing their frequently purchased products as well as a defined product catalog listing only the products they purchase. Customers will be able, for example, to drill down into a product to view spare-part detail and will then be able to order replacement parts online.

Organizations should not underestimate the power of personalization. In online bookselling, for example, Amazon was able to gain an early advantage over both Borders and Barnes & Noble, the industry leaders, largely because it developed excellent personalization capabilities that the two giants were initially unable to match. This early move secured a loyal following of online customers, for whom personalized shopping on the Amazon site became a compelling experience. As Borders and Barnes & Noble are beginning to match the personalization capabilities of Amazon, they are making headway against Amazon's lead in the online channel. But their lateness in responding to Amazon's challenge is a lesson for other organizations, regardless of the industry, concerning the power of personalization in creating customer loyalty.

Personalization has multiple dimensions, and organizations continue to experiment with and extend the ways in which they can use technology to create more intimate customer experiences. But there are several key concepts that organizations should keep in mind as they seek to create personalized experiences for their customers.

Individualize Content

One basic principle of personalization is that content—for example, product information, special offers, and so on—should be individualized for the specific customer. On the Web, this means that what the site visitor sees should be driven by rules based on information about that customer. The effectiveness of these rules depends, of course, on how much information the organization knows about the customer (another reason why "Know the Customer" is the cardinal rule of eBusiness). Amazon.com, for example, uses information about a registered customer's prior book purchases to recommend new books when she logs on to the site. As the customer searches for a specific title, the Web site dynamically generates new lists of recommended books. These recommendations are based on "collaborative filtering" rules: the site dynamically analyzes the purchase data of all customers to determine strong correlations between sales of specific books; the new list of recommendations is introduced with the message "Customers who bought this book also bought ..." This technique leverages preferences of customers in the aggregate to help individual shoppers discover books in which they might be interested but otherwise would not have known about. It mimics the kind of personalized advice that an independent bookseller might offer a patron in the store—and it's also an effective way to sell additional books to Amazon shoppers.

Enable Customers to Customize the Environment

The degree to which the customer environment can be customized largely depends on the medium or channel. Due to its dynamic nature, the Web offers a highly customizable environment. For instance, organizations can enable registered customers to create a customized personal home page on the organization's site. When registered customers log on to the site, the first thing they see is their personalized home page. Customers can set preferences for the content they view—for instance, one customer might want to see daily news for a particular industry on his home page, while another customer might prefer to view the latest sports scores each time he logs on.

In a business-to-business context, the rise of online exchanges presents opportunities for trading partners that participate in these exchanges to customize the exchange environment, in order to accommodate specific requirements of the trading relationship. For example, our client bLiquid.com is the leading auction site for used construction equipment, linking together people who want to buy and sell lathes, forklifts, dump trucks, and other heavy equipment. To run the site, bLiquid.com uses our Siebel eAuction to customize the auction to suit the needs of this particular market. In many cases, for instance, items being auctioned are one-off, one-of-a-kind implements that potential buyers need to inspect before they buy—which makes online auctioning to multiple bidders virtually impossible, since prospective buyers are unlikely to spend the time and money traveling to view a piece of equipment if they are not assured of the seller's commitment. With the eAuction specialized software, bLiquid.com's customers can establish one-to-one negotiations rather than using a multiple bidding format. The software also enables bLiquid.com to offer features such as real-time financing and real-time shipping cost information, which helps streamline the purchasing experience.

Personalization can also be applied to dynamically adjust the content that customer-facing *employees* view as they interact with customers. For example, one of our customers is a leading provider of outsourced call center services, and its numerous clients include organizations from a wide variety of industries. The company's call center agents, therefore, can be dealing with clothing sales one moment and automotive support the next. In addition, the services that the company offers to its customers are different for each customer. One may offer FAQs (answers to "frequently asked questions"), for instance, while another does not. By using our personalization software, the company can adapt the information available to the call center agent, depending on the agent's attributes and identity and on the identity of the calling party. For example, the configuration of the user interface depends on the call center agent's specialty; that is, agents will see different "views" of information and different in-screen applications (or "applets") based on their expertise. Similarly, views and applets dynamically change based on which client's customers are calling. Call center agents are thus more effective, because the personalization rules place the appropriate information at their fingertips.

Personalize Interactions Through All Channels

Though much discussion of personalization naturally focuses on Web-based interactions, it is important to realize that organizations can and should use eBusiness technology and processes to personalize all contacts with a customer, no matter through which channel the interaction occurs. Marriott, for example, maintains detailed profiles and transaction histories of its repeat customers; when a repeat customer calls to make a reservation, the call-center agent can suggest an individualized itinerary for that guest—a round of golf, for example, or a day at the spa—based on the customer's profile and known preferences. That personalization continues when the customer arrives at the hotel and is greeted by name at the front desk, picks up his or her individual itinerary, and finds that the appropriate reservations have been made.

Marriott applies personalization to its relationships with business customers, as well, similarly based on its ability to maintain detailed profiles of these customers using our eBusiness software. These profiles contain information about customer preferences regarding meeting-room layouts, audiovisual requirements, meals, recreation, and so on. With this rich information, Marriott is able to anticipate the needs of its repeat customers, enabling it to add value by, for example, suggesting meal plans and recreational activities best suited for a specific business function. This proactive capability not only allows Marriott to save customers time, but it also increases customer satisfaction and loyalty, leading to both greater share of mind and greater share of wallet.

Finally, effective personalization helps to address one of the emerging paradoxes of the eBusiness era. Customers are demanding more choice, and organizations are responding by providing greater variety and mass-customization solutions to product and service offerings—thus shifting an enormous amount of power to customers. The paradox is that while this shift has greatly empowered customers—in that they have a wealth of options to select from—it has also made them need more help, not less, in choosing from this expanding universe of options. Personalization provides a powerful way to solve this rising demand for more assistance, by guiding customers to the specific product or service that most closely matches their preferences.

WorldCom:
From Selling Long-Distance Service to Selling Complete Communications Solutions

By strengthening our relationships with customers, we are positioning WorldCom to be the provider of choice as our customers expand into the next generation of services.

—ELOISE MCNEAL, VICE PRESIDENT OF BUSINESS MARKETS
SALES AND SERVICES SYSTEMS, WORLDCOM

WORLDCOM AT A GLANCE

Founded in 1983 as a long-distance reseller, WorldCom today is one of the world's largest communications companies. The company employs 77,000 people and generated sales of over $39 billion in 2000 across six lines of business: long distance (52 percent of revenue), data (24 percent of revenue), Internet (13.5 percent of revenue), international (6.5 percent of revenue), local (3 percent of revenue), and messaging (1 percent of revenue). The company has operations in North America, Latin America, Europe, and the Asia Pacific region.

Deregulation and globalization, combined with technological innovation, have radically altered the communications market over the past decade. Barriers have consistently been eliminated regarding which services telecommunications firms can provide and where they can compete. At the same time, technology has dramatically changed the way people communicate. Customers once content with basic voice services now seek wireless services, data services, Internet access, and Web-hosting services, among others. In fact, basic voice services are fast becoming a commodity, with price cuts leading to flat or shrinking revenue in the voice market for all major telecom companies.

WorldCom has been working diligently to adapt to the new communications marketplace. Within the last several years, the company has intensified its efforts to become a more business-focused communications company, backed by the strength of its digital and international businesses. CEO Bernard J. Ebbers has been working to restructure the company into a data- and Web-focused, high-growth business, with its voice-based business providing the funds to finance the company's transformation. The company recently created two tracking stocks to reflect this restructuring. The "WorldCom" tracking stock reflects the primary growth businesses within the company—data, Internet, Web-hosting, and international services for corporate customers—while the "MCI" tracking stock reflects the company's high-cash-flow businesses: consumer, small business, and wholesale voice-based long-distance and dial-up Internet service.

The overall strategy of the "WorldCom" business group is to provide a full complement of eBusiness-enabling communications services for corporate customers worldwide. "We're striving to become a complete solutions provider to our corporate customers," says Eloise McNeal, WorldCom's Vice President of Business Markets Sales and Services Systems. "With the complexity of telecommunications today, customers don't want to have to be experts. They want us to be the experts for them. They look to us to bundle together a broad range of telecom, data, Internet, and network services that will help them solve their business problems." To this end, WorldCom acquired UUNET, which provides Internet access options, Web hosting, and colocation services (i.e., hosting and maintaining a customer's communications equipment in a WorldCom data center and providing leased access to a dedicated network). Additionally, WorldCom recently announced plans to jointly market its services with Digex, which provides managed Web-hosting solutions (i.e., creating, hosting, and maintaining a customer's Web presence). WorldCom plans to acquire Digex's parent company, Intermedia, in 2001.

To fulfill its vision of becoming a total solutions provider, however, WorldCom realized that having a broader range of products and services is only half the equation—the other half is having an integrated view of its customers. "To succeed as a complete service provider, we need to have a single view of the customer," says McNeal. "Without this single view, it is difficult to sell collaboratively, understand the full range of opportunities and activities in an account, and provide consistent after-sales service and support. We realized that to achieve our vision of becoming a total solutions provider, we needed a common customer information system for our sales and service community worldwide."

Facilitating Team-Selling Within Global Accounts

While achieving a single view of customers presents a challenge to any organization, it presented an especially difficult challenge to WorldCom. Having acquired or merged with more than seventy companies during its seventeen-year history, WorldCom had hundreds of disparate databases throughout the organization containing customer information. The company needed a robust sales and call center system that would consolidate this disparate customer information and provide a common desktop interface for all sales and service personnel.

The company decided to begin the implementation of its customer information system in its Global Accounts unit. Global corporate customers are the most profitable customers in the telecom business today. WorldCom believed that having a comprehensive customer information system would enable the company to differentiate itself in serving these customers and grow its market share.

Global Accounts sales teams at WorldCom are often composed of sales and service specialists representing different WorldCom product groups. Before the implementation of WorldCom's customer information system, these sales specialists lacked a single view of the customer. Sales personnel representing one product group, such as UUNET, would try to sell their product to a global account without knowledge of the other sales activities taking place in the account. This lack of coordination hurt sales productivity and caused Global Accounts to miss opportunities for selling bundled services.

WorldCom's recently deployed customer information system now provides all 3,100 Global Accounts sales personnel with a unified source of customer data from anywhere in the world. At a glance, they can see all opportunities, activities, and service issues associated with any given global account. This capability fosters team selling and enhances sales productivity by eliminating the time-consuming task of running numerous reports from legacy systems to determine an account's status. Moreover, Global Accounts is currently in the process of integrating its internal sales forecasting application with its customer information system to further coordinate selling activities. This integration will enable Global Accounts to more accurately forecast revenue and more easily share forecasts and report on progress against forecasts around the world.

Creating a "Closed-Loop" Customer Information System

To ensure Global Accounts is achieving a complete view of its customers, WorldCom has placed its Global Accounts customer service center on the same customer information system as the Global Accounts sales force. Having the sales force and call center on the same system ensures that Global Accounts is tracking not only all sales activities associated with its accounts, but also service issues. "You have to provide a 360-degree view of the customer," says Tom Kosko, Senior Manager, WorldCom Business Markets. "Our Global Accounts personnel need to be aware of the activities and service issues going through our service center if we want them to succeed in creating total solutions for our customers."

WorldCom's Global Accounts call center has realized remarkable productivity and service improvements since deploying the customer information system. Prior to the implementation, call center agents used three-ring binders to track customers' account profiles. When a customer called, the call center agent had to page through the binder to find answers to the customer's questions. If the customer had a service request, the agent needed to fill out a paper form and physically route it to a service team. The process was time-consuming, occasionally resulted in lost service requests, and often led to incomplete documentation.

In addition to causing administrative inefficiencies and mistakes, the old system also led to uneven quality levels with respect to customer service. "Customers complained that every time they called they were treated differently," says Becky Christoff, Senior Manager, Global Accounts Customer Care Center, WorldCom. "Agents did not have all customer information at their fingertips, so they were giving customers inconsistent and sometimes conflicting answers."

Today in the Global Accounts call center, computer telephony integration (CTI) ensures that a customer's complete account profile automatically appears on screen before an agent takes a call. The agent can see the customer's entire transaction history and all open service requests, enabling the agent to anticipate the customer's needs. For example, before taking the call, the agent will know that the customer called yesterday with a service request regarding its virtual private network. The agent will be able to provide the customer with an immediate update on the status of the service request—who is working on it, progress to date, time to completion—without troubling the customer for any additional information. "There's nothing worse than calling a customer service center and saying, 'I called yesterday,' only to be told, 'No, I'm sorry, our system shows that you never called,'" says Christoff.

The customer information system also standardizes data-entry procedures and provides scripts to guide agents through their interactions with customers. These features preserve data integrity and ensure that customers receive consistent service and information. If the customer has a service request, the agent can electronically route the request to a service team. The system will automatically remind the agent at a later date to call the customer back to ensure the service was completed and the customer is satisfied. "This capability allows us to be proactive rather than reactive with our customers," says Christoff.

Since bringing its customer information system online, the Global Accounts call center has saved $750,000 a year in paper costs, and improved efficiency by eliminating the need for agents to manually follow up on service requests and search for account and product information by hand. In addition, the customer information system has enabled the Global Accounts call center to support dedicated 800 numbers for customers, which offer them a more personalized experience. "When a customer calls us today on his company's dedicated 800 number, any agent in our center can answer the call and make the customer feel as though our entire call center operates just to serve his account," says Christoff, "even though we serve 1,600 other Global Account customers out of the same facility."

Extending the Customer Information System to National Accounts

Given the benefits the Global Accounts call center and sales teams have derived from having a comprehensive customer information system, WorldCom is now extending the same system to its National Accounts group. National Accounts sales teams are responsible for selling into companies that are a level below Global Accounts in terms of monthly sales volume. Like the Global Accounts sales teams, the National Accounts sales teams are composed of many sales and service specialists representing different product groups within WorldCom. Without a single view of the customer, these teams struggled to sell integrated solutions. Now that the customer information system is being deployed, the 5,000 National Accounts field sales representatives are acquiring the unified customer data they need to engage in team selling. Following the lead of Global Accounts, National Accounts also plans to put its call center on the same eBusiness platform as its sales personnel to ensure it maintains a "closed-loop" view of its customers.

Because Global Accounts and National Accounts will be using the same customer information system, WorldCom will be able to deliver seamless service to its Global and National Accounts customers regardless of which service center they may contact. Christoff explains, "Outside operators often transfer calls to the Global Accounts call center when they should have transferred the call to the National Accounts call center or vice versa. In the past, there was no integration between the two centers, so we were constantly transferring calls back and forth. With everyone on the same system, even if a customer gets transferred to the wrong call center, the agent will have all the information necessary to address the customer's questions and will be able to automatically route any service requests to the right service team. To the customers, it will feel as though they are interacting with a single service center."

Web-Enabling the WorldCom Customer Information System

While rolling out its eBusiness system to its call centers and field sales personnel, WorldCom has also been working diligently to integrate the Web into its customer information system. "We have customers who don't want to talk to a human being," says McNeal. "They want a self-service option and they want to be able to communicate with us anytime they want. If we can't provide customers with the option to communicate with us via the method they choose, they will go to somebody else who does provide that capability."

An example of one of WorldCom's Web-based self-service tools is the "WorldCom Interact℠" Web portal. Interact℠ provides Global Account and National Account customers with Java-based tools to control day-to-day communications network operations, including active network management, service analysis, service ordering, and payment processing. "We give them the same view into our network that we have," says Ron McMurtrie, Vice President of eBusiness at WorldCom. "Control has been opened up to customers, and they can do everything one of our technical representatives can do for them on a pure IP connection."

Interact℠ also makes account information available to all interested parties, not just network administrators. In the past, only telecommunications or data services managers could review usage and bills. Now business managers are also able to view this information and arrange payment or purchase additional products with the site's provisioning tools.

To make sure the site is meeting customer needs, WorldCom regularly tracks and analyzes customer activity. Based on its analysis, the company will soon add a "click-to-connect" application to Interact℠. The feature will allow a user to speak with a customer service representative in one of WorldCom's call centers over a voice-over-IP connection.

WorldCom's comprehensive customer information system will be used to track these interactions, ensuring WorldCom maintains an integrated view of its customers regardless of whether an interaction takes place over the telephone, on the Web, or in person. This consolidated record will allow WorldCom to develop a deeper understanding of its customers and deliver a seamless service experience.

Building an Ecosystem

To further enhance its ability to provide customers with total solutions, WorldCom has developed an "eBusiness Partner Sales Program." The program brings WorldCom together with selected companies such as AppNet, Cisco, EMC, Lucent NetworkCare, and Technology Solutions Company to offer sophisticated technologies, application solutions, and development services, as well as database, network integration, hardware, software, and consulting services through a single point of contact. By creating this ecosystem of companies familiar with each other's products, services, and operations, WorldCom reduces the complexity of network design, simplifies hardware and software procurement, and ensures smoother implementation for its customers.

Lessons Learned

Although WorldCom is still in the process of fully deploying its customer information system, the company has learned many valuable lessons regarding the deployment of an eBusiness system. Four of the most important lessons are as follows:

- Collaboration is key.
- Pick your partners carefully.
- Integration takes extra effort.
- Accept failures (limited to non-mission-critical functions).

Collaboration is key—McNeal emphasizes the importance of having customers and internal end users involved in all aspects of deploying an eBusiness system. "If we don't have our customers and end users involved in design and deployment of our eBusiness applications, we won't be successful—period," says McNeal. "We need to have a high degree of interaction with all stakeholders to ensure we deploy applications that meet our users' and customers' needs." When deploying its call center system to the Global Accounts call center, for example, WorldCom's IT department worked closely with call center agents to develop requirements for the system. The IT department then demonstrated prototypes of the system to the call center agents, gathered feedback, and refined the system before rolling it out. When developing Interact^{sm}, WorldCom also involved external customers to ensure that the system was easy to use and met customers' requirements.

Pick your partners carefully—Companies must do their homework before choosing their technology partners, including a thorough check of customer references. "There are a lot of off-the-shelf eBusiness applications out there that are simply not very good," says McNeal. "It is imperative that you do your homework before you come to any agreement with an external partner to license their software." As part of its due-diligence activities, WorldCom visits other companies that have deployed the technology under consideration to see how it is being used. During these visits, WorldCom interviews technical professionals and end users in the host companies to assess the value of the technology and determine which components of the technology would deliver the greatest benefit to WorldCom.

Integration takes extra effort—"Integration will be key to the success of any eBusiness deployment," says McNeal. "It will also be one of the hardest things to do." To this point, McNeal advocates using eBusiness applications that have a track record of integrating seamlessly with other IT systems. She also advocates using "vanilla software"—that is, not customized—as much as possible to speed the integration process and facilitate easy upgrades. Without seamless integration between systems, customer satisfaction will suffer. "Suppose a customer orders something on your Web site and then discovers it's not what he really wanted, so he phones the call center. The last thing he wants to find out is that the agent can't see his order because the Web and call center systems are not integrated," says McNeal. "If the company's systems are not integrated, customers will soon become frustrated and ask, 'Why would I want to order anything else from this company? They clearly don't have their act together.'"

Accept failures (limited to non-mission-critical functions)—McNeal advises companies to test the efficacy of eBusiness applications on a limited scale before deploying the applications across the enterprise. This practice enables a company to avoid mission-critical failures and invest heavily only in those applications that deliver the greatest business benefit. WorldCom has developed a methodology it refers to as "Stage 1-2-3" to guide its technology deployments. Stage 1 is the "market entry" stage, in which a system is prototyped on a small scale in a non-mission-critical function to test its feasibility and value. Failures in this stage are acceptable as they have minimal impact on WorldCom's business. If a system shows promise in Stage 1 and passes WorldCom's technology evaluation, the company moves to Stage 2, also called the "scalability" stage. The primary objective of this stage is to buttress the prototype to support usage on a wider scale. Failures in this stage should be rare given the thorough testing done in Stage 1. Provided that the system operates effectively at greater scale, WorldCom will move to Stage 3, which it refers to as "industrialization." In this stage, the system is rolled out to all business functions and integrated with the rest of WorldCom's IT systems. Failures in Stage 3 should not happen given the checkpoints built into earlier stages.

Looking Ahead

As competition in the communications industry continues to intensify, WorldCom's comprehensive customer information system will play an increasingly important role in supporting the company's "total solutions" strategy. The system empowers WorldCom's sales specialists to sell collaboratively, enables call center agents to deliver superior service, and ensures that the company maintains a closed loop of customer information across all points of customer contact—including face-to-face, over the telephone, and on the Web. The net result is greater customer satisfaction and more opportunities for WorldCom to extend its relationship with customers. "As the complexity of telecommunications products and services continues to increase, customers will want a provider who can solve their issues for them," says McNeal. "By strengthening our relationships with customers, we are positioning WorldCom to be the provider of choice as our customers expand into the next generation of services."

CHAPTER TWELVE

Principle Four: Optimize the Value of Every Customer

This principle operates on two levels. On the macro level, it means focusing on the strategic use of resources to extract maximum value from every customer relationship. On the micro level, it means focusing on maximizing the value of every individual customer interaction. Both aspects are important factors to superior marketplace performance, and eBusiness capabilities can enable organizations to excel on both levels.

Micro Level: Optimize Every Interaction

Every interaction with a prospect or customer is a potential "moment of value": it is both an opportunity to create value for that prospect or customer—by providing excellent service, for example, or selling a needed solution—and an opportunity to receive value, by generating revenue, moving a prospect closer to a purchase decision, strengthening customer loyalty, or achieving some other beneficial result. Therefore, organizations should structure their processes and systems to fully exploit these moments of value.

Specifically, organizations should design their customer-touching processes based on three objectives for every interaction:

- delight the customer with superb service
- generate revenue through intelligent efforts to cross-sell, up-sell, or re-sell

- capture one or more elements of useful information about the customer

By achieving at least one of these objectives with every interaction—and sometimes all three—the organization builds its success one interaction at a time. And ultimately, an organization's overall success is the sum of the value it derives from each of its interactions with customers.

To illustrate the importance of a well-functioning customer interaction process, consider the experience of Murphy Brewery, an Irish maker of beers and lagers owned by the Dutch brewing giant Heineken N.V. A self-commissioned survey indicated that the company needed to enhance its level of customer service. "The main issue was that customers were presented with various points of contact within our organization without any one individual taking responsibility for a specific order, query, or request," recalls Denise Burke, Customer Service and Administration Manager at Murphy Brewery. "Customers found that their requests and queries often went unresolved." The brewery implemented an eBusiness solution by building a dedicated call center to handle all customer inquiries. Now, when a call comes into the center, the agent can quickly identify the customer and view all relevant information about the account, including the customer's purchasing history for the preceding thirteen weeks. This enables agents, for example, to detect when a customer places an order for less than the usual amount. "More often than not," says Burke, "by highlighting that change, the customer reviews and increases their order. In this way, our staff is not only providing excellent service—they are building sales."

Many if not most organizations are not optimizing their existing customer relationships, because they are capturing less than the full potential of customer wallet share. Typically, the root cause is that the organization does not have a comprehensive view of the customer or has not captured information upon which it can base effective cross-selling, up-selling, and re-selling strategies.

In a public sector context, another of our clients, the nonprofit American Heart Association (AHA), faces the problem of fragmented information limiting its potential to derive maximum value from its base of six to eight million donors and nearly four million volunteers. The organization has more than sixty disparate databases of donor and volunteer information spread throughout its U.S. operations. Because it is difficult to view donor and volunteer data in a consolidated fashion, the AHA cannot fully leverage this information to support its cause of fighting heart disease and stroke. Efforts to solicit donations are not always coordinated, and donors are not targeted as effectively as possible: for example, affluent donors may receive a variety of appeals from different parts of the organization, rather than one request tailored to their specific interests and capacity to give. In addition, with donor contact occurring across several different communication channels—the Web, the call center, local offices, and in the field—keeping staff apprised of the different aspects of a particular donor's involvement is a time-consuming and manual process.

All of these factors add up to a less than optimal use of a key asset: the donor and volunteer base. To solve these problems, AHA is implementing a comprehensive information system to consolidate all donor and volunteer information and make it readily accessible throughout the entire organization. The system, which is being rolled out in phases to the AHA's dozen different business units, will enable the organization to track all donor and volunteer interactions, their interests, and their donations. As a result, for the first time AHA will be able to analyze its existing donor base and develop donor profiles to better market its fund-raising efforts.

Another way to gain greater wallet share from customers is to offer an expanded menu of marketplace options, such as an online auction. This tactic proved successful for The Sharper Image. In 1998, The Sharper Image decided to step up its Internet strategy through an expanded eCommerce presence, which contributed to a large portion of its overall growth as a company. However, suboptimal inventory turns, cross-selling, and price targets for unique items were still challenges for the company's eCommerce operations—and it also desired to create stronger online customer relationships. In 1999, the company launched an online auction using our Siebel *eAuction* software to complement its existing eCommerce store. Not only has the auction capability driven more traffic to the company's site, but it also enables The Sharper Image to utilize customer bidding information for promotional and cross-selling opportunities. The net result is higher revenues through the selling of excess and refurbished goods.

Macro Level: Optimize Lifetime Customer Value

From the macro-level perspective, optimizing the lifetime value of the customer means spending just the right amount on acquiring and retaining that customer—no more and no less—so that the organization realizes its targeted rate of return on those investments. To optimize its investment in a customer, an organization needs to estimate how much a customer is worth—not only today, but over the entire time period in which the customer will do business with the organization. This estimate is the lifetime value (LTV) of the customer.

Though the rule sounds simple enough, it has profound implications for the way in which an organization must think about its customers. For example, it requires the organization to think in terms of customer relationships instead of transactions, and to take a long-term view of these relationships. Customers provide revenues not only from the initial transaction but from all future transactions as well; indeed, at any given point in time, all customer value exists in the future—and the organization's ongoing task is to figure out how to allocate resources to extract maximum customer value at minimum cost.

The innovation that eBusiness brings to this fundamental task is the ability to optimize the problem at the customer-specific level: that is, the eBusiness system enables the organization to capture and analyze fine-grained, customer-specific data; create robust models of expected customer behavior based on those analyses; and apply those models to finely cut customer segments—even to specific customers or accounts.

How does an organization calculate the LTV? The basic methodology begins by analyzing detailed customer purchase and internal cost data to calculate:

A. average duration of customer tenure in years (on average, how long does a customer remain a customer?)

B. average number of transactions in each year of customer tenure
   (on average, how much business does the customer transact with
   the organization each year during that tenure?)
C. average profit per each transaction.

For each year of the customer tenure, multiply B times C to calculate
average profit per year. Then apply an appropriate discount rate to each
year's profit (to account for the time value of money—i.e., the fact that
any given amount of money is worth less a year from now than it is
today), and sum the discounted yearly profit figures. The result is the
LTV: if the organization spent just this amount to acquire and retain the
customer, it would break even. So the LTV provides a benchmark figure
for the organization to guide its allocation of resources across marketing,
sales, service, and other processes required to build and maintain customer relationships.

Note that this analysis requires calculating customer profitability separately for each year of the customer tenure. This is because, in many
industries, customer transactions change significantly over time, and to
be accurate the LTV should reflect this fact. Of course, the effect of these
patterns on the LTV calculation depends both on the magnitude of the
year-to-year variation in transactions and on the number of years. In
markets where customer tenure is long (more than three years) and
annual spending varies significantly, the effect on the LTV calculation
will be pronounced; it will be less significant in markets where customer
tenure is typically short and yearly transactions are fairly constant.

The LTV calculation presented above is an extremely simple
approach; in reality, most organizations must use a significantly more
sophisticated model to calculate LTV. The simple model described here,
for example, calculates the LTV for the "average customer," by lumping
together all customer data and deriving a single value. A more sophisticated model will distinguish among different customer segments (or
profiles) to develop separate LTVs for each one. To do this, the organization performs the same analysis—that is, determines average duration,
number of yearly transactions, and profit per transaction—but does
this for each relevant customer segment or profile type. This enables
the organization to optimize LTV at a finer level: it now knows, for

example, that it can profitably spend more to acquire and retain customer A than customer B, and therefore can adjust its marketing, sales, and service strategy and offerings accordingly.

Another item that should be factored into LTV analysis is the value of referrals from established customers. For example, if the organization concludes that one in four customers generates a referral, then the value of that referral should be reflected in the LTV (that is, in this example, the LTV should include an additional 25 percent of a full customer value to reflect the one-in-four referral rate). Modeling the referral factor can take a more sophisticated and fine-grained approach. For instance, the organization may observe significant time-related patterns in referral behavior.

One eBusiness Leader's Experience

Telstra Corporation:
From Old-Fashioned Monopoly to
Customer-centric eBusiness

*In the distant past, we didn't have customers, we had subscribers.
We were a monopoly and people simply subscribed. There was
no other game in town. Over the last decade we have moved to being
customer-focused and now the customer relationship is paramount.*

—NEGBA M. WEISS-DOLEV,
DIRECTOR OF E-PROCESSES AT TELSTRA

TELSTRA AT A GLANCE

Telstra is the number-one telecommunications operator in Australia.
Telstra provides local, long-distance, and international telephone
service, with about 7 million residential lines and more than 3 million business lines. The carrier also has 3.8 million mobile phone
customers. Telstra provides business data communications and is Australia's leading Internet Service Provider, with nearly 500,000 subscribers. Telstra also competes in Hong Kong, Japan, New Zealand,
and the United Kingdom. Other businesses include pay TV (through
50-percent-owned Foxtel) and directory services. The Australian
government owns 50.1 percent of the company.

Few companies have faced more changes in recent times than Telstra
Corporation. In little more than a decade, the company has gone from
being the sole provider of products and services in the Australian

telecommunications market to facing competition from over thirty-five licensed carriers, over 100 telecom service providers (e.g., mobile service providers), and 850 Internet service providers. In addition, within just the last three years, the company has gone from being a state monopoly to having 49.9 percent of its shares publicly traded.

The company was first subjected to competition in the national and international long-distance service markets in 1991. By 1992, it faced competition in the mobile telephone service market. Australia's regulatory climate was further liberalized in 1997 to allow for open competition, with no limit on the number of telecommunications carriers that could enter the market. At the same time that deregulation was increasing competition, customers' requirements were changing dramatically. Previously satisfied with little more than "fixed-line" voice carriage, customers were increasingly seeking wireless services, enhanced data carriage capabilities, and Internet-related services. Telstra's competitive landscape was changing from all directions: customers had many more needs, a plethora of options for meeting those needs, and higher expectations for quality and service than they ever had in the past.

In order to survive in this new environment, Telstra felt that it would need to expand the range of products, services, and solutions it provided to customers. To thrive, on the other hand, Telstra believed that it would need to fundamentally transform its relationship with its customers. "Clearly, we've been investing a lot of money into the Internet, into the IP carriage business, and into wireless networks," says Peter Frueh, Telstra's Executive Director of Indirect Channels for retail operations. "But increasingly, we're finding that value is provided by the long-lasting customer relationships that we build and our ability to personalize the customer experience." For Telstra, implementing a customer-focused eBusiness system has proven critical to achieving this vision.

The Early Stages of Telstra's Transformation

Well before implementing an eBusiness system, Telstra began to take steps to transform its relationship with customers. In 1994, the company created a set of values that recognized that the customer was paramount in everything the company did. "The Customer Comes First" became the number-one item on Telstra's list of seven core values. The company backed its commitment to the customer by providing its employees with extensive training aimed at equipping them with the skills and creating the attitudes necessary for delivering outstanding customer service. "We started out by providing training that would help people be more pleasant on the phone, more responsive, and more polite," says Negba Weiss-Dolev, Director, e-Processes. "We tried to communicate that customers now had a choice and will vote with their money. We communicated the fact that we were no longer a product company; we were a customer service company."

Training and communication aimed at creating a customer-centric culture continued throughout the 1990s, and management remained tireless in communicating the importance of being customer focused. The following excerpts from Telstra's annual reports from 1995 to 1999 provide a high-level view of this ongoing attention to the customer:

1. 1995 CEO's Overview: "We are operating in an increasingly competitive environment, with strong pressures to retain and win back customers. . . . Telstra is preparing to tackle this challenging environment by: continuing to strive for a high level of reliable, quality customer service. . . ."

2. 1996 CEO's Overview: "We have achieved much in recent years, including a cultural transformation to customer orientation. . . . As we continue with the cultural transformation of the Corporation, we wish to be (and be seen as) not only a highly competitive, technology-smart market leader, but also an approachable and friendly company—one which is easy to do business with . . . and one which is responsive to customer and community needs."

3. 1997 CEO's Overview: "Adding value for our customer base is our driving force, and the ideal of service and the drive for improvement must be at the core of the culture of the organization."

4. 1998 CEO's Overview: "Over the past twelve months one of our primary tasks has been to maximize the value of your

investment in the company through excellent customer service, development of new products and services, and focus on cost control."
5. 1999 CEO's Overview: "The last, and by no way the least important, part of our strategy is the transformation of our corporate culture and improvement in productivity and customer service."

At the same time that Telstra was focusing on creating a customer-centric culture, the company was extending its lines of business and investing heavily in new technologies, such as its cable network, to defend itself from competitors. In recognition of new business opportunities and to further differentiate itself from competitors, Telstra also invested heavily in building its Internet service provider (ISP) business and its wireless business.

An Inadequate IT Response

Despite having these new lines of business and a more customer-focused workforce, the company's desire to strengthen its relationship with customers remained hampered by an IT system that failed to support customer relationship management activities. For example, Telstra had created its cellular business as a stand-alone operation with its own customer database, which meant that customers often appeared in both the cellular and fixed-line databases. As such, Telstra was unable to gain a consolidated view of its customers, making it difficult to understand the full picture of its customers' needs, preferences, and potential interests in new products and services. Moreover, customers suffered the inconvenience of receiving multiple bills and having to call different numbers for service.

Telstra's IT system also failed to support the company's customer support staff in their efforts to serve customers. "We had really complex products and product descriptions which our front office staff couldn't keep up with," explains Weiss-Dolev. "Our communications weren't synchronized when we'd issue specials. We would advertise a special in the newspaper, but in some cases customer service staff wouldn't know about it in advance."

Weiss-Dolev adds that the lack of synchronization across customer-facing departments made it difficult to resolve support issues. "Customers would ring up with a question or problem and our front office personnel wouldn't have an answer at their fingertips, because the answer could only be found by calling a different department," she says. "Customers would be told to call another number or that somebody would get back to them and that didn't always happen. That lack of follow-up and lack of ownership for problems means that no matter how nice you are on the phone, the customer walks away feeling frustrated."

Telstra decided that to fully realize the benefits of its other long-running efforts to strengthen the company's relationship with its customers, it would need to deploy a dynamic eBusiness system that would allow it to present a seamless face to its customers and unify its customer relationship management activities. "During most of the 1990s, the customer had to know Telstra to be able to work with our systems, and that's not appropriate," says Weiss-Dolev. "The customer had to know which areas to call for different services. You shouldn't have to understand the organization to get the services you need. The organization should understand you."

Building an eBusiness System

Telstra began implementing its eBusiness system in 1999. The system provides the company with the ability to personalize its interactions with customers, offer them choices in the way they interact with Telstra, and synchronize all customer-facing channels, including the Web, call centers, field sales, business partners, and marketing. The company began its deployment by rolling out an eBusiness call center application for its Telephone Account Managers in its outbound call center. "This was where we could most quickly impact our business," explains Ross Riddock, General Manager of Telstra's Business Services Information Technology Unit. "We rolled out account, contact, and opportunity management modules." Greg Sky, manager of the outbound call center, adds, "Within one week of the deployment, we achieved substantial growth in new sales and we've repeated this growth consistently and grown in the following weeks." Additionally, within four months of the deployment, the Telstra account management team achieved a threefold gain in employee productivity.

The success of Telstra's initial deployment led the company to expand its eBusiness system to target four work streams: (1) sales and account management; (2) partner commissions; (3) order fulfillment; and (4) marketing. Based on this strategy, Telstra began implementing eBusiness applications to all of its field sales, call center, telesales, and partner organizations. These applications now provide a common interface for viewing data from more than a hundred back-office and legacy systems, including billing systems. The company expects to have over 4,000 employees using its eBusiness system before the end of 2001. The deployment will improve sales and service effectiveness by giving all Telstra representatives and partners a consistent view that will enable them to better understand their customers' business needs and buying habits and to personalize customer interactions.

Frueh underscores the strategic importance of having this consistent view of the customer: "One of Telstra's business objectives is to move up the 'value tree' in Australia and provide much more in the range of services, content, and solutions to customers, from residential customers right through to our large corporate customers. Only by providing outstanding service will we earn the right to expand our relationship with customers in this way. And we must be able to deliver very high service levels regardless of the customer contact channel that is used."

Frueh adds that the advent of the Internet has made channel synchronization even more important. "If a customer has made an inquiry online at our telstra.com site, then makes a subsequent inquiry over the phone, we would like our customer contact people to be aware of the previous online interaction. Even better, we want our customers to have the option of clicking through from our Web site to speak to a customer contact person directly. If you provide customers with the ability to talk to somebody after they have conducted their own analysis over the Web, you get a very big jump in the number of people who will do a transaction with you."

Weiss-Dolev echoes Frueh's sentiments regarding the importance of having a synchronized multichannel system. She says, "We need to provide as many channels as possible to assure flexibility and nimbleness, but from a customer perspective, the benefit we offer is our integrated services. As a result, we need to integrate our communication channels so they're seamless. No matter if you call me on your cellular phone, from a pay phone, from your home phone, or you get online, I should be able to recognize you as the same customer and have access to the same data, so if you move from one channel to another, I can provide you with continuous service. The fundamental tenet underneath what we're doing is that customers should be able to contact us in any way they choose. We will not force a customer to choose a particular channel. We might charge customers slightly more to use one channel rather than another if we want to direct traffic, but it's ultimately their choice."

Telstra's next step in building its eBusiness system will be to integrate its resellers and channel partners into the system by deploying a Web-based partner portal. Over the next few years, Telstra expects to grow its reseller and partner business to 50 percent of its total sales. The partner portal will allow Telstra to manage its partners as extended sales and service organizations, ensuring that it maintains a seamless view of the customer across all points of interaction. The portal will enable Telstra to manage opportunities, accounts, and service requests of the appropriate channel partner and then track performance on all assigned items. In addition, the portal will ensure that dealer commissions are paid accurately and on time, strengthening the bond between Telstra and its channel partners. Telstra also plans to deploy a new order-fulfillment eBusiness application that will allow customers to configure and place their own orders, resolve billing inquiries on their own, and simplify the process of tracking orders.

Alongside Telstra's efforts to develop a multichannel eBusiness system to better manage customer relationships, the company has also been striving to use the Internet specifically to streamline its internal processes and interactions with suppliers. In March of 2000, Telstra formed the e-Processes Directorate, which is headed by Weiss-Dolev. The Directorate is charged with driving the strategy to Web-enable not only customer interactions but also the management of Telstra's supply chain, and the work of Telstra's business support staff, by December 2001.

Lessons Learned

Telstra believes there are several important issues to keep in mind when implementing an eBusiness system. According to Frueh, one of the first things a company needs to do is establish clear priorities. "The extent of what you can do with eBusiness applications is enormous," he says. "The key is to understand which eBusiness applications are most important to your business." Weiss-Dolev adds, "Making the transition to e-commerce and e-processes is quite often miscategorized as a technology and tools issue. What's hard to achieve is clarity of the questions to which you need solutions. No one can do that clarification for you—you really need to achieve focus and clarity on what it is you're trying to achieve and set some priorities."

Second, Telstra advocates using out-of-the-box software whenever possible. "If we could take software that required no customization, we would do it," says Frueh. "Vanilla software increases the speed of implementation and makes ongoing software support much easier. We very much wanted to adapt our systems to a best-practice model rather than modify a best-practice model to fit our system."

Third, Telstra advocates choosing applications that can support a multichannel system and implementing these applications in phases. "You need to have applications that will support interactions across multiple channels or you won't get the full benefits," says Frueh. "But you don't need to implement a full suite of applications to get started. We started by using an eBusiness call center application in just one call center and we experienced tremendous benefits. Pick the right part of your business, build your experience, and extend the applications from there." Frueh adds that implementing too many applications at once can be challenging for customer-facing personnel. A phased rollout scheme accompanied by appropriate training ensures that staff members are able to use the eBusiness applications to deliver maximum value to customers.

Finally, Telstra has found value in working with an eBusiness applications vendor that develops products for multiple industries and can share this multi-industry knowledge with Telstra. "We liked the fact that we could leverage our vendor's multi-industry R and D," says Frueh. "There are certain practices that exist in other industries such as insurance that we may want to carry across to our own industry. Vendors that only provide solutions for a single industry cannot bring this multi-industry knowledge to the table."

Having focused for nearly a decade on creating a customer-focused culture and extending its lines of business to better serve customers, Telstra's eBusiness system is proving to be the cornerpiece in the company's effort to truly transform its customer relationships. The company produced double-digit profit growth for the financial year ending in June 2000, and it continues to maintain a 50 percent share, or better, in all market sectors except the Internet. With its powerful eBusiness system coming online, the company will be well equipped to keep its customers delighted, its competitors at bay, and its profits growing in the years to come.

CHAPTER THIRTEEN

Principle Five: Focus on 100 Percent Customer Satisfaction

Why should organizations focus on 100 percent customer satisfaction? Why not some other measure, such as revenue growth? Because complete customer satisfaction is a leading indicator of customer retention: properly implemented, an organizational focus on 100 percent customer satisfaction acts as an "early warning system" to detect weaknesses that cause dissatisfaction and, ultimately, loss of customers to competitors. Though organizations must carefully track financial performance—revenue, profit, average order size, and so on—these metrics are lagging indicators of the quality of customer relationships. By the time an organization sees its profits or sales growth drop, for example, dissatisfied customers may already have defected to the competition.

If, however, the organization closely and continually monitors and measures customer satisfaction, it may have both the time and information to better address the needs of dissatisfied customers and prevent their loss to competitors. (A methodology to measure, monitor, and track customer satisfaction is described in Part III.) In addition, evidence indicates that increased customer satisfaction leads to increased revenues. A study of the linkage between customer satisfaction and revenues at Sears, Roebuck, for example, found that each 1.3 percent increase in customer satisfaction boosted revenues by .5 percent.

There are two senses to the meaning of "100 percent customer satisfaction," both of which are important to an organization's success in attracting and retaining customers. First, it means that the organization must strive to satisfy 100 percent of its targeted customers: these are the customers whom the organization has selected to serve, customers who fit the organization's value proposition. The implicit idea is that not all of an organization's customers are desirable: an organization cannot be all things to all customers, and it should not waste resources trying to satisfy customers who, for example, cost more to serve than the value they return. At one retail bank, for example, 10 percent of the bank's customers actually subsidized 60 percent of its customers, who produced a net loss for the bank. Under these circumstances, it was a mistake for the bank to shift resources away from its high-value customers in order to keep its loss-producing customers satisfied. Instead, the bank either should have created an offering for low-value customers that produced a profit, or it should have actively avoided acquiring those customers in the first place. But in order to devise a marketing strategy to target only high-value prospects, the bank would first need to understand the specific attributes of high-value customers—knowledge that can be systematically gained only with sophisticated eBusiness capabilities.

In some industries, the economics of customer acquisition require that the organization carefully assess the profitability of the potential customer before entering a relationship. This might entail, for example, studying a prospect's various risk characteristics, such as credit risk. In the insurance industry, for instance, insurers typically will absorb a net loss on new policies in the first three or four years. (Part of that loss is explained by the front-loaded commissions paid to insurance agents, who receive a large portion of their total commission in the early years of the policy's term.) Then, in the following years, customer profitability turns positive. Clearly, therefore, insurance companies cannot afford high rates of "churn" (customer loss); only by retaining customers for an optimal length of time can they produce acceptable rates of return. Hence, insurers carefully assess the risk profile of prospective customers before underwriting a policy, including analysis of factors that might indicate a high risk of churn.

The second meaning of "100 percent customer satisfaction" is that organizations should focus on completely satisfying their target customers. This concept comes as news to many organizations, which regard "satisfied" and "completely satisfied" customers as in the same category. But research indicates that merely satisfied customers are far less loyal to an organization than customers who are completely satisfied. Thomas O. Jones and W. Earl Sasser, Jr., writing in the *Harvard Business Review,* reported that at Xerox, for example, "totally satisfied customers were six times more likely to repurchase Xerox products over the next eighteen months than its satisfied customers." And according to a study of retail-banking depositors cited by Sasser and Jones, "completely satisfied customers were nearly 42 percent more likely to be loyal than merely satisfied customers." Based on their research, the authors conclude: "Except in a few rare instances, complete customer satisfaction is the key to customer loyalty and generating superior long-term financial performance."[12] With eBusiness capabilities, organizations can finely track the precise level of satisfaction among their customers and distinguish between satisfied and totally satisfied customers.

Understand the Factors That Delight Customers

By focusing on 100 percent customer satisfaction, organizations can determine which attributes of their products or services matter the most to which of their customers. To do this, organizations must actively solicit customer feedback and analyze the data in fine detail to extract meaningful cause-effect linkages. This information often surprises organizations—and without concrete information based on analysis of actual data, organizations can easily waste resources by making incorrect assumptions about which factors customers truly value. For example, George Day, a professor at the Wharton School, describes one such miscalculation in his book *The Market-Driven Organization:* "A bank set an objective of reducing its teller wait at peak periods to two minutes, yet research showed that any investment to reduce the wait time below four minutes had little leverage."

The factors that delight customers obviously vary from context to context, but certain elements consistently improve customer satisfaction across the board. Empowering customers with self-service capabilities, for instance, is almost certain to enhance customer satisfaction.

Understand the Key Elements That
Build Customer Loyalty

The specific elements that drive loyalty vary, of course, from market to market, from segment to segment, and from customer to customer. But research on the dynamics of customer loyalty indicates several general requirements of any approach to create loyal customers.[13]

Basic value. In offering any product or service, the organization must deliver a basic minimum value: car makers, for example, must produce cars that meet fundamental quality and reliability standards.

Trust. When an organization makes a promise of value to a customer, then keeps that promise, the customer learns to trust the organization. The level of trust escalates through repeated cycles of the "promise made–promise delivered" exchange.

Commitment. Beyond securing the customer's trust by delivering on promises made, organizations must persuade customers that they are committed to serving the customer's needs. Communicating that sense of commitment is a major challenge, but organizations that excel in retaining loyal customers proactively create processes and policies designed to do precisely that. If the customer perceives that the organization is genuinely committed to serving his needs, the customer is likely to reciprocate with a sense of commitment toward the organization.

Enhanced value. To secure and further cement relationships with these committed customers, the organization extends its value proposition by offering additional services, personalized attention, and other enhancements that reinforce customer loyalty. Brokerage firms, for example, reward their most loyal customers with enhanced advisory services, discounts on transactions, preferred access to special deals, and a high degree of customized personal attention.

Anticipation of customer needs. An organization that is firing on all cylinders—that offers basic value, keeps its promises, communicates its commitment to the customer, and extends its value proposition through enhanced services, personalized attention, and the like—achieves the highest levels of customer loyalty and satisfaction by anticipating its customers' needs. This requires, of course, that the organization knows its customers well enough to accurately anticipate their needs. The insurance company, for instance, that tracks key events in the lives of its policyholders—by regularly communicating with policyholders and soliciting this information—can proactively propose additional coverage triggered by these events. The young couple that has their first child, for example, may want to add a life insurance policy to the auto policy they now carry; they may also be interested in an investment vehicle to prepare for their daughter's future college tuition. As the insurance company continues to follow life events of this family, it can take action at key moments: the daughter turns sixteen and gets a driver's license, for example, triggering the insurer to call with an offer to add coverage for her on the couple's auto policy.

In order to proactively focus on 100 percent customer satisfaction as a specific objective, organizations must develop appropriate standards for measuring satisfaction. In addition, organizations can build into their eBusiness system the processes and mechanisms for monitoring those metrics. For example, Honeywell Aerospace, one of the largest aerospace equipment manufacturers in the world, designs, manufactures, markets, and services hundreds of products found on virtually all types of aircraft flying today. The Honeywell unit has developed a proprietary "scorecard" of customer satisfaction metrics, which are tracked and stored by its eBusiness system based on our sales software. According to Honeywell, this customer satisfaction monitoring system is a key component in the company's goal of becoming a customer-driven, sales- and marketing-oriented technology company. Deployed globally to more than 1,400 users, the system enables both Honeywell sales representatives and managers to closely track the level of customer satisfaction and to take action accordingly.

Develop Metrics to Measure Specific Drivers of Loyalty and Satisfaction

Only by measuring the specific drivers of customer loyalty and satisfaction can organizations effectively know when and where to concentrate resources or intervene if need be. Dell Computer has one of the most sophisticated approaches to tracking key drivers of customer loyalty, and even has a "customer experience council," composed of senior executives from each major line of business and reporting to a vice chairman, that focuses on these measurement efforts. Among the loyalty drivers Dell tracks are order fulfillment, product performance, and postsale service and support. For each of these drivers, Dell has developed a specific metric that it regularly measures and monitors. With respect to order fulfillment, for example, the metric is "ship to target," which measures the "percentage of order delivered to the customer on time with complete accuracy." For product performance, the metric is "initial field incident rate" (that is, the "frequency of product problems encountered by customers"), and for service and support the metric is "on-time, first-time fix" (the "percentage of problems fixed on the first visit by a service rep who arrives at the time proposed").[14]

Marriott International: Managing Customer Demand

Marriott International is focused on leveraging eBusiness systems to drive customer service, profitability, and growth.

—MIKE DALTON, SR. VP FOR MARRIOTT LODGING SYSTEMS

MARRIOTT INTERNATIONAL AT A GLANCE

Marriott International is a leading hospitality company, with over 390,000 rooms, spanning more than 2,000 properties, 57 countries, and 13 lodging brands. In addition to its hotels, Marriott also manages senior living communities and services, wholesale food distribution, and procurement services. The company has approximately 151,000 employees and generated systemwide sales of $19.8 billion in 2000. Marriott's presence is so extensive that it is estimated that 8 out of 10 business travelers stay at a Marriott property in any given year.

In 1999, Marriott International won half of all the J. D. Power & Associates awards for the hotel industry. While such accolades would thrill most companies, they represent merely a stepping-stone to a company that aspires to be one of the world's top brands. Since 1997, the world's leading hotel company has been steadily transforming itself from a property-based organization into a truly customer-centric organization, supported by a powerful eBusiness system.

Marriott was the first company in its industry to adopt demand forecasting and yield-management systems, and offered a popular frequent-traveler program many years before competitors. A focus on consistent, outstanding service allows the company to earn the highest customer preference. With these advantages, Marriott already had higher occupancy than its competitors in 1997, but the company wanted to drive total property revenue still higher and achieve even greater customer satisfaction. Unit expansion continued to be a major focus as Marriott improved the distribution of its lodging brands, but eBusiness offered an opportunity to do more with the large number of existing hotels. The company's key measure of success shifted from revenue per available room to revenue per available customer.

Marriott's eBusiness Strategy

Implementing an eBusiness system became central to Marriott's vision of shifting from a property-centric to a customer-centric organization. Marriott wanted a system that would (1) allow the company to manage all customer touch-points across all channels of interaction; (2) establish a unified set of customer data to drive all customer-facing applications and interactions; and (3) offer customers a highly personalized experience based on a rich profile of information. With these goals in mind, Marriott created a five-part eBusiness strategy:

1. Focus on establishing and enhancing long-lasting customer relationships—embrace the customer.
2. Sell the way customers want to buy.
3. Build brand loyalty and awareness across all hotel brands.
4. Derive competitive advantage through customer-focused systems, not property-based systems.
5. Cross-sell additional products and services.

Moreover, this strategy is geared toward Marriott's global operations, not just its U.S. operations. "Any software we bought or any supplier we did business with had to be global," says Mike Dalton, Senior VP of Marriott Lodging Systems. "We wanted the same system globally so we could execute our vision consistently around the world."

1. Focus on establishing and enhancing long-lasting customer relationships—embrace the customer. Throughout the early 1990s, Marriott had viewed the hotel as a product and had primarily employed a reactive sales approach at each property. Marriott realized that if it could learn more about its accounts and store that information, it would be able to anticipate their needs and shift to a more proactive sales approach. To this end, Marriott's eBusiness system was designed to allow its sales teams to collect information on their accounts, manage contacts, record leads, and share opportunities. Armed with this information, Marriott sales representatives can build lasting relationships with their accounts and represent all the hotels in the Marriott portfolio. They can service the account globally rather than just selling rooms at an individual property.

In addition, Marriott is in the process of creating a "consolidated inventory" of its function space across all Marriott properties, meaning all Marriott function space information will be stored in a common database. Before implementing this system, the information required to perform sales and event bookings was contained in decentralized systems located at each hotel, making it difficult to coordinate selling and service efforts across the organization. With the new consolidated inventory, sales representatives in every distribution channel can sell space at all properties. As a result, when a trade association based in Washington, D.C., needs to arrange a three-part trade show in Washington, Tokyo, and Singapore, it only needs to call a single sales associate to make all its arrangements. Furthermore, having a single view of function space inventory will allow regional sales offices to close sales during the customer's initial phone call. According to Dalton, "Because Marriott sales associates will have all the information at their fingertips, they'll be able to close a sale while the customer is still on the phone."

Marriott's owners/franchisees comprise another important customer segment that Marriott's eBusiness system enables the company to embrace. Almost all of Marriott's 2,000 properties worldwide are owned or franchised by one of hundreds of independent companies. To effectively manage its relationships with these companies, Marriott must track approximately 2,500 contacts and stay abreast of 500 potential development opportunities at any given time. These development opportunities can take the form of new hotels that are going to be built from the ground up or hotels that could be converted to the Marriott brand. Marriott's total financial performance is heavily dependent on the performance of its owners/franchisees, so serving them well is paramount. Unsatisfied owners might very well decide to build a competitor's brand rather than a Marriott on a new site.

Given the importance of these customers, Marriott developed an Owner/Franchise Relations application within its eBusiness system to make it easier for owners/franchisees developing new hotels to do business with the company. As an owner develops a property, he must interact with several departments within Marriott, including legal, architecture and construction, finance, operations, and human resources. Before developing the Owner/Franchise Relations application, the information across Marriott's departments was not shared in a common database, which resulted in a lack of coordination and confusion. The construction department, for example, may have changed the opening date on a new hotel without informing the operations and human resources departments, resulting in extra delays and frustration for owners/franchisees. With the new Owner/Franchise Relations application, all associates working with owners/franchisees share data regarding everything from construction schedules to new development opportunities associated with the given owner/franchisee. Marriott has streamlined the entire process of interacting with its owners/franchisees and has boosted the satisfaction of these critical customers significantly.

2. Sell the way customers want to buy. Another important aspect of Marriott's eBusiness system is its support of interactions with customers across multiple channels. Currently, Marriott handles over a million reservations per week through a variety of channels, including the phone, the Web, travel agents, and in person. A customer may make a reservation on the Web, then call Marriott's 800 number to adjust the reservation, and finally arrive at the hotel with a desire to modify the reservation yet again. Without an integrated eBusiness system linked to a common database of customer information, Marriott would never be able to deliver seamless service across all of these interactions.

"We need to be able to service our customers consistently, regardless of which channel they use to reach us," says Dalton. "Currently, about 3 percent of systemwide reservations are made over the Internet. Even though we expect that number to increase significantly over the next several years, we expect that most of our interactions with customers will continue to take place over the phone and in person. Either way, the information we have about our customers and the information we provide to them must be the same across all channels to ensure a consistent experience. The business traveler, in particular, will come at you several different ways, and they expect you to have the same information and provide the same level of service across the entire chain. This requires a central database of customer profile information enriched with customer preferences, past-stay history, and Marriott Rewards club membership status."

3. Build brand loyalty and awareness across hotel brands. Marriott manages a diversified portfolio of lodging properties, ranging from luxury to economy accommodations: The Ritz-Carlton Hotel Company LLC; Marriott Hotels, Resorts & Suites; Renaissance Hotels and Resorts; Residence Inn by Marriott; Courtyard by Marriott; SpringHill Suites by Marriott; Fairfield Inn by Marriott; TownePlace Suites by Marriott; Marriott Vacation Club International; Ritz-Carlton Club, Horizons; and ExecuStay by Marriott.

With such an array of brands, Marriott wanted an eBusiness system that would help build brand loyalty and awareness across the company's entire portfolio. Before implementing its system, Marriott's sales force logged information in disparate databases depending on the hotels or hotel groups to which they were assigned. If a guest wanted to book a room or a meeting at a hotel that was full, Marriott's reservations systems had no way of knowing whether another Marriott chain in the same city was available. Tony Reid, vice president of sales information and planning systems, says he knows the system has made a difference because Marriott captured $55 million in cross-chain sales last year—a measurement it was not able to track before.[15]

By keeping customers within the Marriott portfolio, the company not only prevents sending business to the competition in the short term, but also gathers increasingly rich information about customers' preferences. This information can then be used to support a virtuous cycle whereby customers receive a highly personalized experience regardless of the particular Marriott brand or property they are visiting.

4. Derive competitive advantage through customer-focused systems, not property-based systems. During the early 1990s, the hotel industry favored decentralized IT systems that focused on local property-based operations. In its strategy to become even more customer-centric, Marriott realized the importance of implementing an eBusiness system focused on customers and their needs—independent of any particular property. To this goal, Marriott's eBusiness system is being developed as a centralized, integrated software suite utilizing a few shared databases. There is broader dependence on the network to deliver timely and enriched data at all customer touch points. This architecture allows Marriott's diverse and geographically dispersed sales team, as well as its regional call centers, to share information effectively across all lodging brands. Marriott Associates can now deliver more responsive, consistent, and timely service to their customers—any time, any place, and through any channel.

5. Cross-sell additional products and service. The fifth aspect of Marriott's eBusiness strategy is its focus on cross-selling additional products and services to its customers in a manner that increases revenue per available customer while simultaneously improving guest satisfaction. For example, Marriott has developed a program called "Personal Planning Service," which allows Marriott to create personalized vacation itineraries for guests at select resorts well in advance of arrival. "The guest experience starts when you are planning the itinerary, not just when you arrive on the property," says Reid. "If a guest has pleasant dealings with a hotel for three weeks before the vacation starts, it's a more lasting memory."[16] When a customer calls and makes a reservation for one of Marriott's select resorts, the company starts building an itinerary based on the customer's requests and stored preferences. When the customer arrives at the hotel three weeks later, tee times have already been scheduled, dinner reservations arranged, and recreation itineraries created. Marriott has found that guests who participate in the program show noticeably higher guest satisfaction scores and spend an average of $100 more per day on services beyond the room rate.[17] They are also more likely to generate repeat business, because they have had a great experience.

Human Resource Practices and Policies

To support its transformation from a property-centric to a customer-centric organization, Marriott has ensured that its human resource practices and policies are aligned with its organizational objectives. In terms of staffing, Marriott has made certain that the teams it creates to work on eBusiness initiatives include both business and IT professionals. "We made a commitment that on any project we would have both business and systems ownership," says Dalton. "We have a business project manager as well as a systems project manager on every project so that we're making decisions that are both functionally and technologically appropriate."

Marriott also evaluates its managers on the basis of customer satisfaction by including customer satisfaction as one of the four measures on its "balanced scorecard." The other three measures are financial performance, market share, and associate satisfaction. To gather data on customer satisfaction, Marriott periodically surveys customers via phone and e-mail, and leaves guest satisfaction surveys in all Marriott rooms. Marriott is moving to include all associates in the incentive-based compensation plan.

The Technology Criteria Marriott
Used in Building Its eBusiness System

In building its eBusiness system, Marriott used a clear set of technology criteria to guide its decision-making process. For example, the company felt it was critically important to choose software that did not require custom development and could be implemented in stages. "We did a software evaluation in the fall of 1997 and looked at three or four options," says Dalton. "Our ultimate selection was driven around the flexibility and ease of use of the software and the architecture of the software. We wanted a system that we could implement quickly, without spending lots of time and resources on custom development. Our system allowed us to implement phase one within three months, the second phase three months after that, and the third phase just six months later."

Equally important, Marriott wanted an architecture that could support multiple marketing, sales, and service applications. Applications such as Personalized Planning Service, Owner/Franchise Relations, and many others are all run on the same integrated system. "We have gotten away from stovepipe initiatives," states Dalton. "The applications are integrated, and the object-oriented design of the system allows us to very easily incorporate new applications."

Marriott also wanted to work with an eBusiness vendor that could support global operations and add value beyond the software sale. Dalton commented, "One of the criteria we used to choose our vendor is that they are doing the R and D and they are adding the capabilities and the features that match where we're headed in the next two or three years, whether in the area of global capabilities or multichannel initiatives. They pull us through our application portfolio rather than us pushing them."

Dalton concludes his evaluation of his company's eBusiness system as follows: "Anytime we look at any type of technology project, it has to meet at least two or three of our technology decision criteria: (1) it must improve business profitability; (2) it must enhance customer value and loyalty; (3) it must support simplification and integration of business processes; (4) it must reduce technology costs; and (5) it must improve systems delivery and performance. Our eBusiness system has delivered on every single one of these criteria."

Looking to the Future

Marriott is leading the lodging industry in terms of redefining the reaches of customer satisfaction and loyalty. In 2000, Marriott was selected for the second consecutive year as a CIO-100 honoree by *CIO*, the magazine for information executives. The CIO-100 award program recognizes organizations that have mastered the "customer connection" by establishing a strong customer relationship management strategy enabled by eBusiness technology.

The company's hotels are achieving occupancy levels that are typically ten percentage points or more above the industry average due to their ability to deliver more value to travelers of all categories than competing hotels. In various studies, Marriott's customer preference is more than double its nearest competitor. "We want our customers' loyalty to be to Marriott," summarizes Dalton. "When our customers think about travel, we want them to think about us first." With its customer-centric focus and robust eBusiness system, Marriott is well on its way to realizing this ambitious vision.

CHAPTER FOURTEEN

Principle Six: Develop and Maintain a Global, Customer-centric eBusiness Architecture

Without the infrastructure to capture, organize, analyze, and manipulate data, all of the preceding principles are moot. That is, an organization cannot become an eBusiness—cannot know its customers, optimize the use of multiple channels, personalize the customer experience, focus on 100 percent customer satisfaction, and so on—without having the technological foundation to do so. A well-designed system must adhere to several key guidelines:

Store Data in a Centralized Repository, to Create a Single, Unified View of the Customer

From an information technology perspective, the essential component of this architecture is a centralized repository of customer and product information. Though the concept is simple enough, surprisingly few organizations actually have this in place. Typically, they have a patchwork of multiple applications—some homegrown, others purchased from various vendors and modified over the years—along with multiple databases buried in various departments and divisions, all unconnected to one another. Some information, for example, resides in one division's billing system, some in another division's marketing system, and still more on the laptops of individual sales and field service representatives in a third division.

Customer information, however, is most useful when it is consolidated into a single, 360-degree view of the customer. Without this unified view, the organization cannot provide the customer with a seamless experience. This was the problem facing one of Europe's leading commercial banks. As a consequence of the bank having multiple, unintegrated systems that handled various customer interactions, a customer calling the bank might have to talk to several individuals before getting his or her service request resolved, if at all. So dissatisfied were customers by this poor service that some of the bank's large customers were complaining directly to its president and were leaving. To solve the problem, the bank implemented eBusiness software that enabled service representatives to have a consolidated view of both product and customer information, including service request information. The bank integrated the eBusiness applications with its back-office system of record, thus enabling customer service personnel to view customer transaction data in real time. As a result, the bank experienced increases in both productivity and customer satisfaction, and it has also improved its ability to cross-sell products to its existing customer base.

Only by centralizing customer information can an organization achieve a unified view of the customer. Indeed, this capability is the central enabling feature of an effective eBusiness system. Via the global system, personnel in marketing, sales, and service, in any location and in any line of business, can access this single view and gain a comprehensive understanding of the customer.

Update Information Dynamically

Another key requirement of the system architecture is that it should update information dynamically, in real time. That is to say, as customers interact with the system—whether online, via the call center, through an in-store purchase, and so on—that information ought to be immediately recorded by the system, in the customer's file. This is an important aspect of channel synchronization. For example, if a customer places an order on the Web, then telephones the call center later with a question about the order, the service agent should be able to view all the details of the

Web-based order. (Similarly, the cross-channel synchronization should work the other way around as well: the customer should be able to view, via a self-service Web page, details of an order that he made through the call center.) With their expectations conditioned by the best customer service organizations (such as Charles Schwab & Co.), today's customers expect the same quality of seamless experience from every organization with which they do business.

In a fully implemented eBusiness system, this dynamic updating not only occurs throughout the organization but also captures relevant interactions of partners with common customers. For example, if a Compaq reseller is servicing a systems-down environment, then the Compaq field sales representative who is about to call on that account to try to close an order needs to know about the service status before making the sales call. Organizations can extend their eBusiness capabilities to their channel partners using eBusiness software that enables them to track channel partner interactions with common customers.

Modify the System on the Fly

In addition to dynamic updating capability, the system architecture also requires the ability to be modified on the fly, in order to reflect changes in the organization's business rules and practices. This capability is greatly simplified if the architecture provides easy-to-use methods for designing workflow rules and assigning tasks. Rules and practices can change over time—often evolving gradually but sometimes changing abruptly—and the eBusiness system needs the flexibility to adapt to these changes easily and with minimal disruption. The types of possible changes are myriad:

- Sales territories are reconfigured and reassigned.
- Product configuration rules are modified, with new components and models replacing discontinued ones.
- New marketing promotions and special promotions reserved for certain classes of customers constantly come online—often with complex rules restricting their applicability in conjunction with other offers—and then they expire.

Organizations must be able to quickly modify their eBusiness systems to incorporate these strategic and tactical adjustments.

Integrate with Back-Office and Legacy Systems

Ensuring a high level of customer satisfaction depends both on the processes that touch the customer directly—such as sales and service—and on back-office processes that may not directly touch the customer but nonetheless affect the quality of the customer experience. For example, when a customer orders a product online, execution of that order depends on the right information being communicated to the back office, which will trigger a number of additional processes, such as fulfillment and billing. The online ordering system, therefore, must be integrated with the fulfillment, accounting, and distribution systems—and all of the associated information should be accessible via a common interface to the various parties who may need to view it, including the customer. At Federal Express, for example, a customer can check the exact status of a shipment simply by entering the airbill number on the FedEx Web site.

Integration with back-office systems also is critical to the deployment of real-time configuration and price quoting capabilities. For example, one of our customers is a leading supplier of highly complex communications and networking products and services. We are working with the company to integrate its configuration system with its back-end Oracle Manufacturing software. By using an integrated combination of our sales and configuration software, the company's mobile and inside sales representatives can now browse the product catalog, with or without the customer, and can accurately configure orders and quotes. The configurator application serves as the central repository of product data, pricing data, business rules, and product relationships. The company intends to extend this configuration capability to several hundred channel partners, giving partners a Web-based means to configure orders and quotes online. In addition, the company can allow its customers to access this information via a Web-based application. Thus the eBusiness solution can extend across all of the company's channels, from the customer all the way to manufacturing.

Solving the back-office integration problem can produce dramatic benefits in the call center as well, as demonstrated by the recent experience of our client State Industrial Products, a leading U.S. specialty chemicals supplier to the maintenance industry. Its call center agents were working with paper-based calendars and customer records, along with computerized access to order-entry screens based on SAP software. As a result of this cumbersome system, customer callbacks were not getting made and leads were not being followed up on in a timely manner. In addition, agents found the SAP-based order-entry interface very unwieldy. When a customer called, agents could not view a single, comprehensive view of the customer account—a situation that impeded effective cross-selling and up-selling opportunities. By implementing our call-center software, integrated with a State Industrial's SAP back-office system, the problem was solved.

Now its agents can quickly see what tasks they have to complete on a daily basis, eliminating untimely callbacks and lost leads. Moreover, because computerized customer records can be easily accessed, all the old paper-based files have been removed. Product information is stored in the new system, which agents now use for order entry, rather than the SAP screen. The streamlined system has greatly simplified order entry, and agents now have both the information and tools to effectively up-sell and cross-sell. In fact, the call center has now become the most profitable department of the company.

Ensure That the System Is Extensible and Scalable

The pace of business continues to accelerate, which means that the ability to react to change is more important than ever. As a result, as an organization evolves and grows, so must its eBusiness architecture. From a technology perspective, the architecture must be flexibile in two key respects. First, it must be extensible—that is, it should have open "application programmatic interfaces" (APIs), so that it can be easily integrated with other packaged and custom-built applications. Second, it must be scalable—that is, it should be able to handle tens of thousands of concurrent users accessing databases housing several hundred terabytes in volume, all without falling below an acceptable threshold of transaction processing time.

Support All Applicable Platforms and Devices

Today's organizations take advantage of a broad range of information and communications devices, including mainframes, desktop PCs, laptops, handheld devices, pagers, and cell phones. A state-of-the-art eBusiness system, therefore, must extend to all of these devices, whatever the underlying hardware and operating systems, and must work seamlessly across all devices. Like any system, the global eBusiness system is only as robust as its weakest link. For example, users of mobile devices such as laptops and handheld computers must be able to easily and effectively synchronize information stored locally on their device with the system's centralized database. Without this capability, mobile personnel are not working in sync with the rest of the organization, a situation that can create negative customer experiences. At one major electronics company, for example, field sales representatives did not have an effective way of tapping into the latest customer and product information stored in the company's corporate database. As a result, representatives sometimes had the embarrassing experience of calling on customers who had better information than the representative, because the customer had phoned the company's headquarters to get the latest information before the representative came to visit.

In the pharmaceutical industry, where field sales personnel must have access to essential information such as drug data and physician profiles, leveraging the use of handheld devices is especially productive. In the United States, for example, one of our customers, DuPont Pharmaceuticals, Inc., needed to provide its sales representatives with a tool for profiling targeted physicians and accounts on demand. In particular, the company was not able to arm sales personnel with previous call history and call notes at the point of interaction. So DuPont deployed software specifically tailored for the pharmaceuticals industry that synchronizes call history and profile information to each representative's handheld device. As a result, representatives can strategically plan their calls in the field and provide a more targeted message to individual physicians. That kind of ability will increase physician satisfaction and help drive product prescriptions.

Support Global Implementation, with Multiple Languages and Currencies

To be truly global, an eBusiness system must support the languages and currencies in every location in which the organization does business. And it must accommodate changes in those situations (such as the introduction of the euro in Europe). As organizations continue to extend their geographic reach and global footprint, their eBusiness systems must be able to match that growing globalization.

Present Customers with a Single View of the Organization

Just as the organization seeks to provide its customer-facing personnel with a single, unified view of the customer, so too should it provide customers with a unified view of the organization. This means, for example, coordinating all communications to customers to avoid sending conflicting messages. It also means presenting a seamless public presence to customers and enabling them to communicate with the organization in a streamlined way.

Many organizations fall short on these criteria. In the automobile industry, for instance, car makers collectively spend billions of dollars each year to create strong manufacturer brand identities. Yet their distribution channels—that is, the independently owned franchised dealers—do not necessarily reinforce the manufacturer's identity: customers perceive dealers as separate, fragmented entities that only partially represent the manufacturer. A common frustration for car buyers, for example, is the general lack of coordination among dealerships. If one dealer doesn't have a model that a particular customer wants, that dealer has to phone other dealers to find the desired car. Meanwhile, the customer loses patience and wonders why there isn't a better system.

Saturn Corporation, an emerging eBusiness leader in the automotive industry, is addressing this and other distribution issues by investing $300 million in the Saturn Next Generation Retail System—a comprehensive Web-based information system that will link all 400 of its retail facilities nationwide with each other and with customers and partners. An estimated 15,000 retail team members will use the system to view vehicle inventory anywhere in the Saturn network in real time and to communicate with customers, fielding questions and tracking special needs. The system will also make it easier for consumers to do business with Saturn dealers: customers will be able to connect to the system over the Internet, for example, to schedule service appointments and check the service history on their vehicles.

By synchronizing all channels and points of contact—showroom, service department, and corporate Web site—Saturn can provide customers with a highly integrated experience. The customer can connect with any dealer, and each dealer has access to that customer's history—no more islands of information. For Saturn customers, each dealer will be an extension of a seamless corporate presence.

Honeywell International, Inc.:
Enhancing the Customer Experience

*Nothing is more important in achieving our growth ambitions than building
and sustaining strong customer relationships. That's why we are striving
to build a customer-centered culture in the new Honeywell. In today's
competitive world, companies that do the best job of delighting customers
consistently achieve better financial results than their competitors.
We are determined to be one of those companies.*

—HONEYWELL 1999 ANNUAL REPORT

HONEYWELL INTERNATIONAL AT A GLANCE

Honeywell International (formerly AlliedSignal) makes a variety of
products for aerospace, automation, power, and transportation uses,
generating sales of $25 billion in 2000. The company also makes per-
formance materials used in semiconductors, polymers for electronics
and carpet fibers, and specialty chemicals. About 40 percent of Honeywell's sales come from aerospace products, which include turbofan
and turboprop engines and systems for flight safety and aircraft land-
ing. Its automation segment (26 percent) includes industrial and
home controls for heating and ventilation and for manufacturing
processes. In October 2000, General Electric announced plans to
acquire Honeywell in a tax-free merger, and Honeywell shareholders
approved the merger in January 2001.

The "new" Honeywell took shape in the fall of 1999 with the merger of
AlliedSignal and Honeywell, Inc. The deal created a $25 billion manufac-
turing and services conglomerate with more than 120,000 employees in

nearly 100 countries. As separate entities, AlliedSignal had a reputation for excelling at internal productivity processes, whereas Honeywell was viewed as better at delighting the customer. Nevertheless, both companies were highly focused on the traditional drivers of bottom-line performance for industrial companies: continuous improvement of manufacturing processes; tightly focused R&D; and minimization of fixed assets, working capital, and head count. This focus helped AlliedSignal and Honeywell grow year-on-year net income at 15 percent and 20 percent, respectively, during the four years before the merger.

Sales growth, however, was less than inspiring and showed only a 5 percent increase during the first year of the "new" Honeywell—not enough given the company's goal of achieving annual sales growth of 8 to 10 percent.[18] To achieve this goal, the new Honeywell is focused on using its large installed base to capture more business from existing customers. In addition, the company is moving from a price-driven product strategy to a value-driven solutions approach. Solutions businesses command higher margins, require less asset intensity, and deliver ongoing service revenue. Nothing is more important in Honeywell's growth strategy than building and sustaining customer relationships. By strengthening customer relationships, Honeywell believes it will win more business from existing customers and earn the right to provide customers with complete solutions. One of Honeywell's primary strategies for strengthening customer relationships has been to implement a customer-focused eBusiness system.

eBusiness Within the Honeywell Industrial Control Business Unit

A strong example of how Honeywell is using eBusiness applications to strengthen customer relationships is found in Honeywell's Industrial Control (HIC) business unit. The $2.5 billion HIC business unit provides advanced control software and industrial automation systems for industrial customers ranging from chemical to pulp and paper companies. According to Rob Baxter, VP and CIO of Honeywell Industrial Control, customer satisfaction has become the number-one driver of competitive success in his business today. "Customer satisfaction has become crucial because product differentiation is increasingly difficult to achieve. Honeywell has a very large installed base, and the cost of acquiring a new customer is very high, so customer retention and an expansion of the existing customer relationship is of paramount importance. The world has changed. Our business model has turned upside down, and to be successful, we must redeploy our assets to focus on the customer interface and on the ever-increasing demands our customers are placing on us. We must find a way to capitalize on this new environment, or we will find ourselves left behind." Baxter uses the following diagram to illustrate the essence of Honeywell's redeployment of assets:

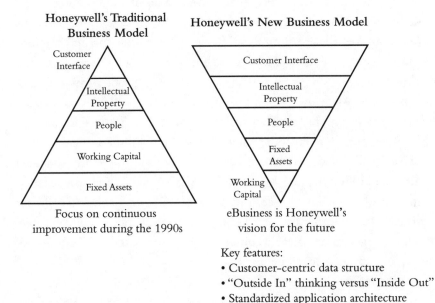

Honeywell's Traditional Business Model	Honeywell's New Business Model
Customer Interface	Customer Interface
Intellectual Property	Intellectual Property
People	People
Working Capital	Fixed Assets
Fixed Assets	Working Capital
Focus on continuous improvement during the 1990s	eBusiness is Honeywell's vision for the future

Key features:
• Customer-centric data structure
• "Outside In" thinking versus "Inside Out"
• Standardized application architecture

Knowledge Management—A specific example of how HIC has redeployed its assets to focus on customers is through its "Knowledge Management" initiative. HIC has built a knowledge base over the years of solutions to the many types of problems that occur in manufacturing plants. Until recently, however, much of this knowledge remained "tribal knowledge" as opposed to "institutional knowledge." In other words, the knowledge resided in disparate databases or in the minds of service personnel around the world rather than in a central database. As a result, when a customer called a HIC service representative with a problem, the service representative rarely had an answer at his fingertips. Typically, the service representative had to contact a technician, who in turn needed to query separate customer, call history, and technical databases for an answer. In the event an answer could not be found, the technician had to dispatch someone from field support to fix the problem. The problem-resolution time in such a scenario could be eight hours or more. Moreover, there was no systematic way of storing the newfound solution in a comprehensive repository that would make the knowledge accessible to others in the future.

To rectify this problem, HIC implemented an eBusiness application that consolidates solutions to over 50,000 problems in a common database and makes those solutions available to everyone in the "support chain"—from call center agents to technical assistance center agents to field technicians. "Our goal is to never discover a problem twice," says Baxter. "Once we've discovered a problem, we communicate it to everyone in the support chain so they are aware of it. That way, if the problem starts to occur at a customer site, it can be identified quickly and resolved." Additionally, customers have Web access to the entire database, so they can often resolve problems on their own. International customers find this self-service option especially valuable. As Baxter explains, "If a customer has a problem in Singapore, they need to be able to get the right information as quickly as possible without having to go through a whole series of people that they may not know."

HIC now has more than 4,000 customers in more than 60 countries using its online service application. The business unit also has 3,600 field engineers using the new application to expedite problem solving. In fact, since launching the online service application, HIC's problem resolution time has dropped from 8 hours to approximately 20 minutes for problems profiled in the database. If customers are not able to resolve a problem on their own using the site's knowledge base, they can submit service requests on the site, update service requests, and add attachments to a service request further explaining the problem. In addition, the application allows customers to fill out a customer feedback survey for each service request, helping HIC ensure complete customer satisfaction. If customer satisfaction levels fall out of tolerance—that is, a satisfaction rating of less than 4 on a scale of 1 ("very poor") to 5 ("excellent")—HIC has a documented process for addressing the low rating and will escalate the problem to the HIC executive team if it cannot be expeditiously resolved.

Because HIC's online service application is synchronized with the rest of HIC's support chain, the business unit has been able to significantly increase customer satisfaction while simultaneously streamlining its service infrastructure. "Customer delight" has risen from 92.3 to 98.1 percent since implementing the online service application, while HIC has been able to trim its call center staff by 15 percent and its call center managers by 30 percent, and reduce the number of databases from 17 (isolated databases) to 4 (integrated databases).

Extranets—To strengthen its relationships with its strategic accounts (e.g., Shell, Exxon), HIC has taken "knowledge management" to yet a higher level. It has established extranets with these customers to track all interactions between the HIC and the accounts. According to Baxter, this tracking of interactions has allowed the strategic accounts to gain valuable information about their own internal operations. "They're finding out about things happening in their company that they weren't even aware of, such as new product introductions, the status of beta tests, and inter-company management meetings and pricing agreements," explains Baxter. "Our strategic customers are leveraging the data stored on these extranets to avoid duplication of effort and better track the full range of activities taking place within their own organization."

HIC's strategic accounts can also use the extranets to learn about industry best practices. HIC engages in joint research with its strategic accounts on various topics related to industrial control—such as the most profitable way to extract airplane fuel during the oil-refining process—and then makes the research available to all strategic accounts over the extranets. This joint-development work allows the strategic accounts to gain access to a wide range of research on industry best practices while sharing the cost with the rest of HIC's strategic customers. HIC benefits by becoming the knowledge center for the entire industry, which greatly strengthens the bond it has with customers. "You have to keep recrafting your relationship with customers," says Baxter. "You have to keep building a tighter and tighter relationship, because customers' needs are changing at a faster pace all the time. As soon as your relationship with a customer stops growing, you open yourself up to being displaced by a competitor. For example, Honeywell and other automation systems providers were traditionally product suppliers, but by working closely with our customers, we migrated faster than other product suppliers to the role of a value-added service provider. If you don't stay close to your customers, this migration will occur without you, and you will be left behind."

MyPlant.com—To enhance its relationship with customers outside its strategic accounts, HIC has created "MyPlant.com." The site serves as a unique, Web-based resource for plant managers, engineers, and operational staff seeking solutions to help them solve plant problems and improve operational performance. According to Baxter, "MyPlant.com grew out of a very creative, forward-looking effort to understand our industrial customers' needs and satisfy those needs as effectively as we could." The electronic hub provides visitors with direct access to a global community of leading industry consultants, software providers, academic professionals, and engineering service firms. Not only is the site itself a revenue source—customers can download demo plant configurations for a very small fee—it is helping HIC build brand preference and reach potential customers that would have been almost impossible to reach pre-Internet. Small customers who cannot afford expensive licensing fees can essentially rent Honeywell's intellectual property. Moreover, the site exemplifies how a company can strengthen its relationship with customers by integrating strategic partners into its ecosystem.

Excelling at eBusiness

One of the most important success factors for eBusiness is having a customer-centric culture, and Honeywell has taken many steps to create such a culture. One of the most significant has been its Six Sigma initiative. Six Sigma is a quality-improvement and business strategy that employs statistical and problem-solving tools to reduce defects, cycle time, and costs. The statistical and problem-solving tools are similar to other modern-day quality-improvement strategies. However, Six Sigma stresses the application of these tools in a methodical and systematic fashion to gain knowledge that leads to breakthrough improvements with dramatic, measurable impact on the bottom line.

Some of Honeywell's businesses have been using Six Sigma methodologies since 1995. When AlliedSignal and Honeywell merged, the companies blended the best of their respective quality programs to create Six Sigma Plus. This new approach was decidedly customer-driven and aimed to make the company better at listening to customers, anticipating their needs, and solving their problems. Six Sigma methodologies began to be applied to sales, marketing, and service processes rather than simply to manufacturing processes. For example, Honeywell began using Six Sigma tools to improve the rate at which it converted sales quotes into closed orders.

In addition to Six Sigma Plus activities, Honeywell engages its customers on a regular basis to discuss their needs. For example, several hundred customers attend each of HIC's annual user group meetings in Europe, Asia, Latin America, and North America. "There's a tremendous amount of information exchange about products, services, and strategic direction at these meetings," says Baxter. "The exchange of information takes place between Honeywell and its customers as well as between the customers themselves." Throughout the year, HIC also distributes publications to its user groups containing current information about HIC's products, services, and solutions.

To further enhance its relationships with key customers, Honeywell has created dedicated "Strategic Account Alliance teams." These teams are composed of a Honeywell executive and several Honeywell technical experts who partner with an executive and several experts from the customer company. The teams look for ways to enhance value to the customer, eliminate unnecessary costs, and strengthen the relationship between the two companies. Occasionally, they even engage in joint development to create new technologies or services for the customer.

Honeywell also systematically measures customer satisfaction, setting customer satisfaction targets for every project and conducting post-project surveys to assess performance. To ensure accountability, all senior executives at Honeywell have approximately 10 percent of their compensation linked directly to customer satisfaction levels.

Rotating eBusiness champions from division to division is another approach Honeywell takes to ensure the company excels at eBusiness. "We move eBusiness evangelists throughout the company," explains Baxter. "The goal is to seed people who believe in eBusiness and have proven successful at it, so they can serve as catalysts for eBusiness wherever they go in the organization and broker partnerships between managers and information technology specialists." In addition, Honeywell tracks every one of its eBusiness initiatives at the corporate level. "We know exactly how many initiatives we have, what we're spending on them, and the financial returns or the customer satisfaction improvements we're getting out of each one," says Baxter.

Implementing eBusiness: Lessons Learned

Given the company's eBusiness experience to date, Honeywell has learned that one of the most important requirements for implementing eBusiness is executive support. "The senior executives have to get the bug," says Baxter, "and it will come in one of two ways: either they will see a tremendous opportunity or they will be scared to death. It doesn't matter which one brings them around, as long as they become the champions for eBusiness." To ensure eBusiness at Honeywell has continuous executive support, the company has a corporate VP of eBusiness as well as a VP of eBusiness within each of its divisions. The corporate VP is responsible for developing and championing Honeywell's overall eBusiness strategy, while the divisional VPs are responsible for aligning spending, project plans, and deliverables with the corporate strategy.

Honeywell has also learned the value of standardizing the organization on one eBusiness platform. Baxter explains, "If we didn't have a standard application for eBusiness, we would never be able to capture knowledge and share it globally. If you put your information in your little homegrown system and I put my information in my little home-grown system and then we say, 'Okay, now we want to put it on the Web,' the two of us cannot even be sure that we share the same definition for a customer. The other thing is that once you have an eBusiness standard and you capture the information internally, you can turn that information around and make it available to customers."

Honeywell advocates investing the time and resources necessary to train people on the strategic reasons for eBusiness and on how to get the most out of the eBusiness applications they will be using. Implementing an eBusiness system can represent a significant organizational change, and like all changes, it must be managed with care to ensure its success. As such, Honeywell applies its Six Sigma Plus methodology to all eBusiness initiatives to ensure they are as systematically managed as the other activities in the company. For example, prior to launching its online service application, HIC used Six Sigma tools to document the process it was using for handling service requests. It used this documentation as the basis for designing the improved process currently in place, and continues to use Six Sigma tools to monitor and improve upon the process.

Looking to the Future

Honeywell believes that its eBusiness initiatives to date represent just the beginning of its transformation to a fully customer-centric business model. "We're working very hard on the customer-facing end, but it's much harder to rework the back-office systems to be customer-centric," says Baxter. "We originally configured these systems to be internally focused, so it is not the application but the user design that is flawed. The systems have been designed around internal departments like order entry, manufacturing, billing, and so forth. We need an information flow that is horizontally integrated across all of these functions, from sales right through after-market support. We also have a lot of work to do to expand our e-ordering model from one pilot product to all product lines so customers can configure products themselves, generate quotes, and place orders without any human intervention from our side." Honeywell is also looking to expand extranet services to a wider customer base and enrich the content it provides on its extranets. "Our extranets have only been running for nine months and we're getting tremendous customer feedback," says Baxter. "The challenge now is to keep building content and adding personalization features to ensure that we're constantly strengthening our relationship with customers."

Epilogue

In October 2000, General Electric announced plans to acquire Honeywell. In the press release announcing the acquisition, Jack Welch, Chairman and CEO of GE, commented that the two companies are well matched. "Honeywell's core group of businesses—Avionics, Automated Controls, Performance Materials, and its new microturbine technology—are a perfect complement to four of GE's major businesses," he said. "Not only are the businesses a perfect fit, but so are the people and processes. GE's operating system and social architecture, coupled with both companies' common culture based on the initiatives of Six Sigma, Services, Globalization, and eBusiness are also a perfect fit." Welch could have also mentioned the companies' shared commitment to customers. Indeed, three of GE's nine corporate values focus specifically on customers:

- Create a clear, simple, customer-centered vision . . . and continually renew and refresh its execution.
- Remain passionately focused on driving customer success.
- Live Six Sigma Quality . . . ensure that the customer is always the first beneficiary . . . and use it to accelerate growth.[19]

With these shared commitments, GE and Honeywell are well positioned to bring good things to life for customers and shareholders for many years to come.

CHAPTER FIFTEEN

Principle Seven: Leverage and Extend the Ecosystem

From an eBusiness perspective, the term "ecosystem"—adapted and modified from James F. Moore's usage in his book *The Death of Competition*—refers to the constellation of constituents that are tightly connected via the organization's global eBusiness architecture. These primarily include customers, partners, and employees. In the era of eBusiness, success increasingly depends on the effectiveness of the organization's ecosystem, because competition occurs more and more among ecosystems than among individual organizations. Therefore, organizations must continuously seek ways to leverage and extend their ecosystems.

In the past, tight coordination among ecosystem constituents was very difficult to achieve, because it required extensive sharing of information in real time: most individual organizations, let alone networks of organizations, did not have the infrastructure to capture and share information in this way. With a global eBusiness architecture in place, however, organizations can share essentially infinite amounts of finely detailed information in real time. Even more, organizations can use advanced eBusiness capabilities to coordinate these extended relationships—for example, by employing rules-based processes to manage shared customer opportunities with extended channel partners.

Integrate Customers into the Ecosystem

In the era of eBusiness, organizations must increasingly view their relationships with customers as partnerships. The weakest customer relationships

are based purely on transactions and do not extend beyond the immediate exchange of value; in these cases, the organization has little opportunity to instill loyalty in the customer. At the other end of the spectrum,
the strongest relationships are built on collaborative interdependence,
and include a high degree of trust and commitment. For all organizations, the challenge is to manage relationships so that they move farther
along the spectrum toward collaborative interdependence. The benefits
of doing so can even exceed the economic rewards of customer retention. For example, consider the benefits that Microsoft realized by leveraging its customer base in the development of the Windows 2000
version of its operating system. Microsoft distributed beta copies of the
software to more than 650,000 customers, who provided feedback to
Microsoft valued at an estimated $500 million.[20]

Forward-thinking organizations continuously experiment with
innovative ways to bring customers into the organization's ecosystem.
Direct merchant Lands' End, for example, offers a service on its Web site
called "Shop with a Friend," which allows two shoppers to browse the
site together and add items to a single shopping cart. If one person hangs
up or disconnects, the remaining shopper can invite another shopper to
join, browse, and shop.

Integrate Partners into the Ecosystem

Virtually all customer experiences depend on a network of organizations,
each of which delivers one or more components that affect the overall
experience. When a consumer buys a new car, for example, the vehicle is
one piece of a clustered purchase that may also include financing and insurance. From the customer's perspective, the "car-buying experience" also
involves these other elements. One of our customers, a leading automotive
company, recognizes this reality. It is building a system that makes partner
information immediately accessible to dealers. For example, the carmaker's
finance managers can use a Web browser to download the latest financing
and lease information and financial contracts at the point of sale.

Not only do integrated partnerships address the reality of the "whole
customer experience," but they also enable organizations to gather valuable information about their customers. American Airlines, for example,

realizes that the travel experience does not begin and end with the airline flight. So the company has extensive partnerships with other travel-services providers, such as rental car agencies and hotels. A customer booking a flight through American Airlines can at the same time reserve a rental car and a hotel room. American's customers can include their rental car and lodging preferences, along with their flight preferences (e.g., aisle vs. window seat, preferred in-flight meal), in a profile stored in the airline's reservation system—information that customers do not have to repeat each time they make travel arrangements.

A source of even richer customer information is American's mileage-reward partnerships with credit card companies, in which cardholders get American Airlines frequent flier credits for using the card. By analyzing its customers' credit card purchases, American gets a much broader view of its customers' buying patterns. American can then use that information, for instance, to identify prospects for special promotions such as vacation and tour packages.

Organizations can further leverage the eBusiness ecosystem through proactive management of their channel partner relationships. For example, one of our customers is a major automotive company in North America, which has an extensive network of car and truck dealers. After studying lease renewal information, the company discovered that 75 to 80 percent of its customers let their leases run out rather than renewing at the end of the original lease term. In addition, the company found that customers were not always leasing their next vehicle from its dealers once the lease had expired. In an effort to improve lease retention, the company deployed software to provide dealers with better tools to increase the rate of lease renewals—for example, by providing information to dealers about lease holders throughout the life of the vehicle. Dealers use the tools as a way to stay closer to customers during the lease term, to increase the likelihood that customers will lease their next car from them. Dealers are also using the system to track new opportunities and to check on sales order status.

Integrate Employees into the Ecosystem

Within the typical organization, employees in different functional areas, lines of business, product groups, or other unit structures operate with little knowledge of how employees in other groups are interacting with a common set of customers. At best, these segregated employee efforts simply duplicate one another without harming the customer relationship—but in far too many instances, the customer relationship is negatively affected when employees are not aware of each other's efforts. In addition, the organization is almost certainly missing valuable opportunities to enhance and reinforce the customer relationship through well-coordinated efforts among all employees who interact with customers.

Schlumberger Oil Field Services, for example, the world's leading provider of services to the petroleum industry, organized its 3,000-plus sales, technical, and managerial workforce by product line, serving more than 300 geographic territories. Product line groups maintained separate customer databases, even though they had numerous customers in common. As a result, Schlumberger sales personnel from one product line were not fully aware of sales contacts made by the other groups. Moreover, customers were asked the same questions by sales reps from multiple product lines. Schlumberger came to us to implement a single, unified, comprehensive customer information management system. By bringing these formerly unconnected employees into an extended eBusiness ecosystem, the sales force can avoid duplicating efforts and relieve customers from having to repeat information to multiple sales representatives.

A major benefit of bringing employees into the eBusiness ecosystem is the dramatic productivity improvements that can be achieved through eBusiness solutions. We worked with a major consumer electronics manufacturer, for example, whose sales representatives were spending considerable time on administrative work and what they called "tail-chasing phone time." Selling to leading retail accounts such as Best Buy and Circuit City, the company wanted its representatives to spend more time promoting new products, which required providing the representatives with accurate and timely information about their accounts. To solve the problem, we helped implement an eBusiness solution to map all relevant customer data, which was housed in many different systems, to a centralized database. Representatives can now access information in a logical manner using a simple interface. Because productivity was a key goal, we configured the system so that representatives can view 80 percent of the information they typically need with just two clicks of the mouse. In addition, representatives can get real-time updates of inventory and order status information. And they no longer have to log on to multiple systems to access this information, because the system integrates data from two external vendors. Such instant access to a single source of accurate and timely information enables sales representatives to spend more time promoting products to customers, and less time on administrative tasks and chasing down information.

Chase Manhattan:
The Right Relationship Is Everything

With a relentless focus on the customer, Chase is committed to leveraging its powerful technology to understand customer needs better.

—WILLIAM B. HARRISON, JR., CHAIRMAN AND
CEO OF CHASE MANHATTAN CORPORATION

CHASE MANHATTAN AT A GLANCE

With annual revenue exceeding $30 billion and assets of more than $700 million, Chase Manhattan is the #2 bank in the United States and the #31 company in the Fortune 500. Chase offers commercial, consumer, and investment banking services to clients through offices in some fifty countries worldwide. In the United States, the bank is one of the largest mortgage loan originators and the fourth-largest issuer of credit cards (behind Citigroup, BANK ONE, and MBNA). Chase's network of banks is highly concentrated in Texas and the Northeast. The company owns investment bank Chase H&Q (formerly Hambrecht & Quist). In December 2000, Chase and J. P. Morgan & Co. merged to form J. P. Morgan Chase.

Few industries have experienced more upheaval in recent times than the financial services industry. Globalization and deregulation, combined with the information revolution, have transformed financial services into one of the world's fastest-paced and most innovative businesses. No organization better demonstrates the dynamism of today's financial services sector than the Chase Manhattan Corporation.

The market leader in numerous categories in both retail and commercial banking, Chase has achieved its remarkable record by executing a strategy that focuses on the customer relationship. Indeed, since 1996—when Chase Manahattan and Chemical banks merged to form the current organization—Chase adopted a new corporate tagline that succinctly expresses its philosophy: "The Right Relationship Is Everything." A central component of Chase's ability to put substance behind the slogan is its aggressive use of information technology to manage customer relationships.

Chase's National Consumer Services (NCS) group, one of the bank's three major business units, provides a showcase example of how Chase is leading the industry in the practice of customer-centric eBusiness. NCS accounts for approximately 42 percent of Chase's annual revenue, with the remaining revenue coming from the Global Bank division (44 percent) and Global Services division (14 percent). NCS serves more than 32 million customers with personal banking services such as savings, checking, credit card, loan, and investment and retirement products. To manage its numerous customer relationships, NCS is building an information technology platform guided by a vision of a comprehensive system that will bring the customer into full focus across the entire NCS unit.

Competing for Customers

Focus on the customer is a core value at Chase. In fact, it is the first one cited on Chase's list of corporate values. In today's financial services environment, such customer focus is critical. Competition for customers is more intense than ever before, largely as a result of deregulation. In recent years, lawmakers in both the United States and many other countries have dismantled long-standing prohibitions on competition. In the United States, for example, geographic restrictions no longer block banks from competing across state boundaries. In addition, different types of financial service providers—brokerages, insurance companies, banks, and so on—are entering each other's markets.

Financial services organizations are also being buffeted by another major trend: consolidation. The economics of today's financial services environment favor size. Large organizations can realize substantial cost advantages, for example, by spreading their considerable fixed expenses—

on information technology, real estate, ATM networks, research, and so on—over a large number of customers. In addition, both retail and commercial customers increasingly prefer a "one-stop-shopping" solution for their financial needs. To compete globally, financial services organizations must offer an expanding array of products, from checking accounts and credit cards to brokerage services and commercial loans.

Driven by these economic forces, the financial services industry has seen a growing wave of mergers and acquisitions over the last several decades, as major players expand by absorbing competitors. With increasing scale, however, come two major challenges. First, organizations find it more difficult to manage the quality of customer relationships: the growing number of customers and volume of transactions test the organization's customer-service capabilities. Second, organizations inherit a jumble of legacy information systems.

Chase Manhattan NCS faced such a situation in 1998: since 1980, Chase and its predecessor organizations had completed ten major mergers and acquisitions. As a result of the mergers, combined with numerous departmental deployments of customer information systems over the preceding years, NCS found itself with a complicated infrastructure of legacy applications. These systems were used to manage activities ranging from account opening and ATM access code generation to loan rate calculations. Without a comprehensive profile of each customer, and without the means to share that information with other NCS representatives, the division's sales and marketing professionals required extensive phone and e-mail contact with one another to complete essential tasks such as needs analysis and targeting of promotions. When an existing customer responded to a promotion, NCS call center professionals were challenged to capture data consistent with information stored in other systems and at the customer's home branch, because they were unable to see the data stored in those systems. Moreover, service representatives could not easily access that legacy data to speed the process of opening a new account. Despite the availability of the Web and other channels of communication with NCS, customers might have to wait at least a day for the bank to respond to simple inquiries.

According to Bruce Zimmerman, Senior Vice President of Chase Manhattan NCS's Internet group, that level of service is simply unacceptable today. "I think the change in service expectations within the last twenty-four months is probably comparable to the change in the prior decade," he says. "You must be able to create a service experience that is outstanding and consistent. People used to say it was okay if you got back to them in a week. Today they're not satisfied if you can't get back to them right now."

With these considerations in mind, Chase decided to implement a robust eBusiness system that would elevate the company's ability to serve its customers to a new level. The Customer Opportunity Management (CustOM) initiative was born.

Implementing the CustOM Initiative

The CustOM initiative's stated mission is to provide "the right financial solution to the right customer at the right time." In pursuit of this objective, NCS has begun the implementation of CustOM in its Regional Consumer Banking division. This division comprises more than 600 Chase branches and management offices in New York, New Jersey, Connecticut, and Texas; employs more than 5,500 sales and service employees; and serves more than 4.7 million consumers.

CustOM provides access to a centralized database of customer information to all sales and relationship management staff within the Regional Consumer Banking Division. The eBusiness system is integrated with Chase's legacy service systems and provides the division with a platform for managing the entire customer relationship life cycle. For example, during the presales stage (e.g., the prospecting phase), the eBusiness system enables sales professionals and managers to draw on comprehensive customer data to engage in opportunity assessment, goal setting, campaign management, and precall planning. These capabilities increase the efficiency with which the division acquires new customers and helps the division identify prospects who are more likely to be interested in the division's higher-value products, such as money market and retirement accounts. During the sales interview stage, the eBusiness system provides sales professionals with an engine for assessing the needs of a prospect, supports scripted dialogs and product presentations, and models "what-if" scenarios to help the sales professional work with the prospect on financial planning. These capabilities increase the productivity of the division's sales professionals and help them deliver superior service. During the postsales stage, the eBusiness system automates customer follow-up, which supports up-selling and cross-selling efforts. Meanwhile, marketing teams through-out the division can access the same customer information available in the eBusiness system to develop targeted promotions, and they can capture and monitor response to campaigns and measure effectiveness.

Another important aspect of CustOM is its support of business analysis by any segmentation, including location, product, promotion, and teams. For example, the head of the Regional Banking Division can view a summary report of sales performance across all of the division's 600 branches, then drill down to view performance status at successively finer levels of detail: New York State, then New York City, then a specific branch, and finally a specific sales professional. Other managers within the division have access to subsets of this information, depending on their administrative position. This visibility provides management with the ability to more accurately forecast demand, identify new business opportunities, and address performance issues.

In the future, Chase plans to integrate CustOM with the rest of Chase's channels (call centers and Chase.com) to provide customers with the flexibility to use the communication channels they prefer to get a fast, informed response that reflects the most recent contact between the customer and the bank. Denis O'Leary, Executive Vice President and the head of Chase.com, emphasizes the importance of providing cus-tomers with this flexibility: "We believe that having a multichannel strat-egy is critical, because we think that's the way consumers will want to live their lives. While there may be some small segment of customers who want to do everything over one channel, such as the Internet, we think they make up a very small segment. In fact, most consumers, small businesses, and middle-market companies will want to avail themselves of a wide choice of channels to do different things at different times."

eBusiness in the Global Bank Division

In parallel with the rollout of CustOM in the NCS division, Chase has also rolled out an Investor Relationship Information System (IRIS) in its Global Bank division that is built on the same eBusiness platform as

CustOM. IRIS provides sales and account management professionals
with a comprehensive view of business customers and prospects for corporate and institutional products, such as global custody products (i.e.,
processing cross-border securities trades). The Global Bank has also
deployed an application that allows the division to aggregate data on
prospects and customers into a convenient Web portal shared by Global
Bank sales professionals. As part of this effort, Chase has integrated its
internally developed reporting application with its eBusiness system to
provide all professionals with timely briefings on the events of important
customer meetings and the resulting actions being taken by the bank.

Excelling at eBusiness

To excel at eBusiness, Chase appreciates the importance of having a customer-centric workforce. As Zimmerman explains, "The databases, the
main processing platforms, the contact management, and the content
management applications are all just different components of the overall
technology, but eBusiness is about more than just technology. It's very
much about people and process as well." To this point, Chase has carefully addressed people and process issues as it has implemented its eBusiness system. For example, Chase has invested heavily in education and
training to ensure that employees understand the new technologies
being deployed at Chase. When launching the CustOM initiative, Chase
trained 5,500 employees in NCS on the new eBusiness system over the
course of twelve weeks. The training combined Web-based lessons with
instructor-based training and was customized to allow users to experience the exact look and feel of the Chase eBusiness system. The training
included overview classes for all customer-facing employees in NCS,
and then job-specific training for in-branch support staff and managers.
By the completion of training, the NCS employees reported, on average,
a 90 percent confidence level in their ability to effectively use the eBusiness system to better serve customers.

In addition to investing in training, Chase ensures it excels at eBusiness by regularly tracking customer satisfaction using internal research as
well as research from independent third parties. Key drivers of customer

satisfaction include the extent to which customers feel Chase understands them and values their relationship to the bank, works to resolve their issues promptly, and offers competitive products and services. To ensure accountability, Chase includes customer satisfaction as a key measure of performance on its corporate balanced scorecard, which is used to determine incentive compensation for all executives. In fact, a full 40 percent of the incentive compensation paid to Chase's branch managers is based on customer satisfaction scores.

Lessons Learned

In the process of implementing the CustOM intiative, Chase Manhattan has learned several valuable lessons that apply to any eBusiness implementation. First, eBusiness initiatives need support from the highest levels to succeed. Applying information technology to manage customer relationships involves the coordination of multiple parts of the organization and requires close examination of business processes across all marketing, sales, and service operations. For example, the Retail Banking Division of NCS had to agree on a common sales process model—from presales, to sales interviews, to account opening, to postsales follow-up—before it could begin deploying its eBusiness system. Without strong support from the chief executive to drive action across the enterprise, eBusiness initiatives can fall victim to internal resistance. At Chase, the entire corporation understands the importance that CEO William Harrison places on information technology as a strategic asset in managing customer relationships. As he stated in Chase's most recent annual report, "With a relentless focus on the customer, Chase is committed to leveraging its powerful technology to understand customer needs better."

Second, Chase has learned the importance of involving business users heavily in all aspects of the implementation process, from system design, to testing and validation, to the integration with legacy systems, to user acceptance testing. "Involving business users throughout the process helps ensure that the eBusiness system is ultimately embraced," says Jim Burns, Vice President, NCS Strategic Technology. "However, you must work with business users up front to establish the prioritization criteria that will be used in determining which business requirements will guide the configuration of the eBusiness system. Some business requirements are less important than others in terms of their impact on customer satisfaction and financial performance. You should agree on a clear set of criteria for prioritizing your business requirements so you avoid spending a lot of time addressing requirements that are not going to add a lot of value to the business."

Third, in evaluating eBusiness technology, Chase has learned the value of doing its homework and selecting only proven solutions. Chase understood that in selecting the technology to manage its customer relationships, it was entering a partnership with its technology provider. "We like to work with a leader and create more of a partnership as opposed to a vendor/buyer relationship," says O'Leary. "Our software provider really demonstrated a commitment to this partnership approach. While we're still in the implementation phase with certain components of our eBusiness system, we're making progress and feeling very good about our early results." He adds, "The implementation of our eBusiness system in NCS has been very successful, but it is just a first step. Every customer-facing process in the Chase organization—whether aimed at business or retail customers—is currently, or will soon be, reengineered to ensure we create the best total experience for the customer. We believe eBusiness technology will play a central role in allowing us to achieve this objective."

CHAPTER SIXTEEN

Principle Eight: Cultivate an Organizational Culture Built on eBusiness Excellence and Innovation

Becoming an eBusiness is not a one-time event: it is an ongoing process, in which the organization continuously extends and leverages its people, processes, and technology to achieve the highest levels of customer satisfaction. The drive and motivation to maintain this focus must pervade the organization's culture. A distinct organizational culture happens not by accident but by design and conscious, constant effort.

Ensure Commitment of Top Management

Organizational cultures reflect the values of top management. Unless senior executives place a high priority on the organization's eBusiness strategy, the organization as a whole will not perceive its importance. Therefore, both the words and actions of top executives should reflect a deep-seated commitment to becoming an eBusiness. At organizations that have been early successful adopters of eBusiness, the commitment to eBusiness strategy and innovation has invariably come from the highest ranks—for example, Charles Schwab and co-CEO David Pottruck at Schwab; Michael Dell at Dell Computer; and J. W. Marriott, Jr., at Marriott International. This is not coincidental: transformation into an eBusiness requires both significant change throughout the organization and the ongoing maintenance of a strong organizational culture. Without leadership from the top, an organization can neither achieve nor sustain this degree of change.

Create Incentives That Support eBusiness Goals

Nothing speaks louder to employees, whether senior managers or front-line workers, than how the organization rewards its people. The organization's compensation and incentive structures, therefore, must be aligned with the eBusiness strategy and objectives. This means, for example, that customer-satisfaction scores will carry more weight in the organization's profit-sharing program and that sales force compensation will shift from an emphasis on customer acquisition to customer retention. In addition, the organization may have to reconfigure its commission scheme to support a multichannel strategy. At Cisco, for example, salespeople get paid on orders that come in over the Web or through the call center, because Cisco wants its sales force to drive as much business as possible through these lower-cost channels so that field sales representatives can concentrate on higher-value accounts.

Develop and Maintain a Bias for Action

Speed and agility are essential ingredients of organizational success today. The pace of business is accelerating: products are being brought to market more quickly, while their life cycles are getting shorter. Customers' patience also is growing shorter, as their choice of options expands and their ability to act quickens. In nearly all markets, the window for any opportunity closes faster than ever before.

Organizations are agile by design, not by accident. To improve organizational speed, management needs to create the structure and set the policies that promote swift action. Four key measures are to:

Avoid lengthy analysis. Many organizations, facing the dramatic upheaval being forced by the new competitive reality, tend to get locked into the "paralysis by analysis" syndrome. In the fast-paced era of eBusiness, however, time is the enemy of competitive advantage. The organization, therefore, must balance the need for prudent analysis against the imperative to act swiftly.

Flatten the hierarchy. Information travels faster between the frontline to senior management—and throughout the entire organization generally—the fewer the layers and potential choke points it has to pass. A flattened hierarchy not only accelerates the flow of information, it also enables information to reach executives in more authentic, less-filtered form. Therefore, organizations must review their layers of management and reduce them to the absolute minimum.

Expect occasional suboptimal results and learn from them. A bias for action necessarily means that on occasion efforts will not produce the planned results. Indeed, enlightened managers worry when their organizations are not experiencing enough "failures"—that is, they view this as a sign that the organization is not taking enough risks, and therefore is not pushing the limits of the possible or learning by inventive experimentation. Such managers agree with the view expressed by Schwab co-CEO David Pottruck: "I don't worry about failed projects. I worry about missed opportunities."[21] No manager, of course, welcomes suboptimal results, but in today's fast-changing climate they realize the need to act quickly. Fortunately, managers can mitigate the risk of innovation and of acting on unproven hypotheses by pilot-testing ideas to contain any potential downside. If the results are positive, then the pilot can be quickly rolled out on a larger scale.

Test everything, and test all the time. An eBusiness is by definition a learning organization: a primary role of eBusiness is to extend the organization's ability to better understand its customers, its marketplace, and its own processes. This can only happen if the organization regularly tests its assumptions and experiments with new approaches to marketing, sales, and service. Controlled experimentation, therefore, is an integral component of eBusiness.

Chief Executive Officer as Chief Customer Officer

An idea gaining momentum in some quarters is that organizations create a new position of "Chief Customer Officer" (or a similar customer advocacy role). In an effective eBusiness, however, it is the CEO who is ultimately accountable for looking out for customers: indeed, ensuring customer satisfaction should be one of the CEO's top three priorities. Placing final responsibility for customer satisfaction with the CEO makes customer satisfaction a top priority of every subordinate. Under this approach, customer satisfaction does not exist as a separate department: instead, it pervades every part of the organization and becomes a responsibility of all employees.

Dow Chemical:
Finding a Catalyst for Growth

We believe that if we center all of our thinking—organizational, cultural,
procedural, and technological—around the customer, we will create the
kind of breakthrough thinking we need to achieve our vision of being
the easiest company in the world to do business with.

—MACK MURRELL, GLOBAL DIRECTOR OF DOW'S
CORPORATE CUSTOMER INTERFACE INITIATIVE

THE DOW CHEMICAL COMPANY AT A GLANCE

With sales of roughly $23 billion in 2000, Dow is the leading chem-
ical, plastics, and agricultural products company. Most of Dow's sales
(27 percent) come from performance plastics (polyurethanes, epoxy
products, engineering plastics). Other products include plastics (25
percent of sales), performance chemicals (14 percent of sales), agricultural products (10 percent of sales), commodity chemicals (13
percent of sales), and hydrocarbons and energy (10 percent of sales).
The company has 141 manufacturing sites in 32 countries, employs
41,700 people, and supplies more than 2,500 products. In February
2001, Dow acquired chemical company Union Carbide Corporation.

The Dow Chemical Company is a world leader in the production of
plastics, chemicals, hydrocarbons, and herbicides and pesticides. However, the company has faced a nagging problem over the past ten years:
how to grow revenue. The company's ten-year annualized revenue
growth rate is less than 0.5 percent.[22] Although this figure is quite

respectable compared to other companies in the industry—Dow's top competitor, DuPont, has experienced a ten-year annualized revenue growth rate of minus 2 percent[23]—Dow is determined to energize its top line. In order to do so, it knows it must overcome the long-term trend toward the commoditization of chemical products. Within the last year and a half, Dow believes it has found an answer: get closer to customers so it can transform its relationship with them. "In order to grow, we need to extend our brand from a product manufacturing company to a science and technology solutions company," says Mack Murrell, Dow's Global Director of Corporate Customer Interface Initiative. "And to achieve this vision, we need to place the customer at the center of everything we do."

Phase I: "Earning the Right to Grow"

Dow's focus on putting customers at the center of its operations is the second phase of what has been a two-phased effort to put the company on a fundamentally different growth path. "We really think of where we are today as the second part of a two-part journey," says Murrell. "We called the first phase of our journey 'earning the right to grow.' The focus of that phase was taking a couple billion dollars of cost out of our operations, strengthening our product integration, improving business processes, and streamlining our global business structure. We got really efficient at doing the things we do. We typically benchmark now as the low-cost producer in each of our major businesses."

Dow's cost-reduction efforts allowed the company to boost its average annual return on assets to 6.9 percent between 1995 and 1999, compared to just 2.7 percent between 1990 and 1994.[24] Yet the company's revenue remained virtually flat. It was clear that cost-reduction efforts by themselves would not put the company on a new course. Dow therefore decided in early 1999 that it was time to find new ways to grow. As Murrell states, "Once we earned the right to grow, the focus became *growing*. It was as though we were all dressed up for the big dance and we were ready to dance, but we still weren't dancing."

Phase II: Driving Growth by Achieving
New Levels of Customer Intimacy

The second phase of Dow's growth strategy consists of three main components: growing its established businesses, creating totally new businesses, and driving growth through mergers and acquisitions. Underlying all of these efforts, Dow is striving to transform itself from a producer of commodity chemicals into a solutions company. According to Charles Churet, Commercial Director and a member of Dow's Global Commercial Leadership Network, achieving greater customer intimacy is critical to making this transformation. "Customer intimacy and market intimacy put you in a better position to understand the latent needs of your existing and prospective customers," he says. "Customer knowledge enables you to understand where you can innovate and develop *solutions* that capture greater value than the sale of products alone." To achieve this customer intimacy, Dow has been working diligently since 1999 to transform its culture and build an eBusiness system that will make Dow the easiest, fastest, and most convenient company in the world with which to do business.

Creating a Customer-centric Culture

Creating a customer-centric culture has been paramount to Dow's growth strategy and has represented a significant challenge given the company's heritage as a product-centric organization. Murrell provides this perspective: "Dow's been in existence for something like 103 years. We started because Herbert Dow figured out how to pass electricity through salt water and extract bromine. Then he figured out how to extract chlorine. Then he looked at the residue coming out the exhaust pipe and figured out how to make something else. This process went on and on—Dow didn't waste a single molecule. When you do this for a hundred years, some good things happen. You develop very tightly integrated plants, you become very efficient, and you create a low-cost structure. What you don't necessarily get is a strong customer focus."

To build customer focus into the organization, Dow began an accelerated implementation of Six Sigma in 1999. Six Sigma is a total quality program that focuses on achieving ongoing product and service excellence through the use of specific tools and methodologies. Six Sigma also seeks to create an organizational culture in which people constantly strive for perfection in the way they perform their jobs. Achieving customer loyalty is one of the primary objectives of Dow's implementation of Six Sigma, a focus that has pushed Dow to make decisions on the basis of what customers value, not just on what the company wants to offer. To institutionalize this customer focus, Dow has trained nearly 1,000 employees to be Six Sigma "black belts," meaning they are specially trained to fix the processes and systems that directly affect customer success. "Having these black belts throughout the company is a really big deal," says Murrell. "They ensure that everybody in Dow is constantly focused on customer satisfaction."[25]

Dow's corporate scorecard has also been modified to ensure the organization is customer focused. The scorecard is used to track all key corporate success factors, and a customer loyalty index became part of it in 2000. "We've probably done a thousand 'voice of the customer' sessions in the last year where we've asked our customers what the key drivers of loyalty are," says Murrell. "And now we measure ourselves against those drivers, some of which are 'hard drivers' and others are 'soft drivers.' Examples of hard drivers include whether we deliver the correct product at the correct time, at the correct price, and with the correct documentation. Examples of soft drivers include responsiveness to customer service calls, quality of technical support, and the extent to which Dow shares its knowledge with customers to help them improve their business processes. "

Building an eBusiness System

Alongside its cultural change initiatives, Dow developed and has begun implementing a comprehensive eBusiness strategy. One of the most important components of this strategy is the "customer interface initiative." The core objective of this initiative is to integrate information technology, processes, and resources in a manner that allows Dow to serve its customers better than any company in the world. Dow seeks to sell its products and services to customers no matter how they choose to shop—face-to-face, over the phone, online—and provide superior customer service across all channels.

To this end, Dow is building an eBusiness system that synchronizes the company's channels, so that customers can seamlessly interact with Dow through the Web, call center, field sales offices, and telesales. Dow's primary customer channel is its face-to-face sales force, which includes more than 1,400 salespeople globally. In addition, Dow employs 700 customer service representatives, 50 telesales agents, 110 inquiry support agents, and hundreds of technical support people both in the field and in the call centers.

For the initial phase of the eBusiness implementation, Dow deployed an eBusiness call center application to one of its technical support centers, followed by deployments at additional contact centers. According to Murrell, the success of the call center deployments played a pivotal role in the ultimate success of the eBusiness implementation. "After we had the call centers online, we went to the sales force," he says. "They quickly embraced the system because the customer database was already full of information from our call center rollout."

Dow's customer information is being migrated to one central repository, which will eventually be accessible to the company's entire customer service and sales force through a common desktop interface provided by the eBusiness applications. The applications have been integrated with Dow's SAP back-office system. "Right now, we are in the process of linking our eBusiness applications to our other critical back-office systems such as our global data warehouse, fleet management system, and pricing system," says Murrell. "Our vision is to enable employees who have any interaction with customers to get all the data they need through the eBusiness system."

Synchronizing Interactions Across Multiple Channels

Dow's eBusiness system also enables the company's customers to access the company's MyAccount@Dow service, which provides 24x7 customer service and support over the Web. Dow customers who are registered with MyAccount@Dow can review, update, or add service requests, and search knowledge bases. To achieve personalization, Dow's global businesses have customized MyAccount@Dow to give customers access to information specific to their interactions with Dow.

MyAccount@Dow is integrated with the rest of Dow's customer-facing channels, enabling Dow to consolidate customer interactions that take place over the Web with the rest of a customer's record. This integration of activities across multiple channels represents a major advance in Dow's ability to manage its customer relationships. "Even a year ago, the left hand didn't always know what the right hand was doing," confides Murrell. "In the future, when a customer calls Dow for service, we will know the customer's service history and order status before we even pick up the phone based on the caller ID. And that information will be the exact same information that the customer can access on MyAccount@Dow, so even while we're on the phone we'll be able to say, 'We're happy to help you, but if you have this problem after five o'clock, let me show you another way to get the same answers.'"

Currently, Dow has 5,000 of its customers registered as MyAccount@Dow users. Moreover, the company is continually expanding the features of MyAccount@Dow to include increased order-entry flexibility, real-time collaboration, the integration of customer quality feedback opportunities, and more.

Using Consolidated Customer Information to Serve Customers Better

Dow's consolidated customer information will allow Dow to analyze customer behavior and correlate that behavior to "needs-based segments." These segments will be defined on the basis of sales volume as well as by whether a customer type buys on the basis of price, innovation, or convenience. Dow is in the process of building segment-specific "business rules" into its eBusiness system so that Dow employees interacting with a customer know how to best serve the customer's needs. For example, customers who fall into the "price buyer" segment will be offered lower pricing but not specialized services such as technical support or specialized delivery. A convenience buyer is looking for a competitive price but, unlike a price buyer, might not be willing to do a lot of self-service. For these buyers, Dow will try to simplify interactions with the company by offering such services as inventory replacement.[26]

Creating New Channels and Extending the Ecosystem

Another important element of Dow's eBusiness strategy involves the development of new electronic channels that enhance Dow's relationship with its customers. For example, Dow recently joined with several other suppliers to create "Elemica," a neutral business-to-business (B2B) marketplace specifically for the chemicals industry. Dow has also joined with other manufacturers to create "Omnexus," an online B2B marketplace for the global plastics industry. Both initiatives demonstrate the company's commitment to providing customers with additional options in how to do business with Dow.

Dow's eBusiness strategy also focuses on investing in small and developmental e-commerce companies to expand the ecosystem in which it does business. For example, Dow has invested in SciQuest.com, a B2B marketplace for scientific products; TradeRanger, a B2B marketplace for procurement of maintenance, repair, and operating materials; and Chem-Connect, a B2B marketplace and information portal for chemicals, plastics, and industrial gas buyers and sellers. Dow invests in these businesses to enhance the value customers can derive from the larger ecosystem in which Dow does business, and in which Dow stands at the center.

Implementing a Global eBusiness
Strategy: Lessons Learned

Murrell believes there are several obstacles that must be overcome to build a successful eBusiness system. "First you need a burning platform," he says. "Without a sense of urgency, it will be very difficult to overcome organizational inertia. From Dow's perspective, technology advancements—particularly the Internet—provided that platform. We knew we

needed to change the way we conducted business to remain successful."
Second, it is critical to address the organizational and process changes
required to operate as an eBusiness before implementing any technology. "We determined that we would break the development effort into
chunks, building phase two only after we successfully created phase
one," says Murrell. "Making organizational and process changes in front
of the technology implementation really helps you overcome obstacles
once the technology implementation begins." To this point, Murrell
feels the technology implementation is perhaps the biggest obstacle
organizations face when developing an eBusiness system. Murrell
explained, "We tend to work with a handful of suppliers who are experts
in a particular area. Each brings a certain expertise to the table, and they
all understand the importance of working well together."

Dow selects its technology vendors on the basis of their market leadership. "Our number-one consideration when we choose an application
or software provider is who is going to win in the marketplace," says
Murrell.

Dow also follows three core principles when approaching eBusiness
initiatives: (1) think big, (2) start smart, and (3) scale fast.

Think Big: Starting with a market-driven vision, the company consid-
ers all eBusiness possibilities and evaluates all strategic alliances that are
in line with its growth objectives.

Start Smart: Prior to implementing new eBusiness initiatives, Dow exe-
cutes pilot programs to test fresh ideas, incorporate customer feedback
into the design process, and minimize the risk of disruption.

Scale Fast: Technologies that demonstrate value to internal and external customers are aggressively leveraged by Dow across all of its global
businesses and markets.

While Dow feels it is still at the beginning of its journey to revitalize its
top line, CEO Michael J. Parker believes Dow's eBusiness system and its
drive to get ever closer to customers are playing major roles in the company's turnaround. "By making it easier, faster, and more convenient to do

business with Dow, we are delivering greater customer satisfaction and loyalty, which has a direct impact on our financial performance," he says. "As we continue our transformation from a product company to a science and technology solutions company, we aim to delight customers to such an extent that they never want to look elsewhere for a better supplier."

PART III

How to Become
an eBusiness

CHAPTER SEVENTEEN

The Five-Step Methodology

In pursuing an eBusiness strategy, every organization is motivated by a unique set of circumstances: different market environments, competitors, resources, opportunities, and so on. Nonetheless, the experience of hundreds of eBusiness pioneers suggests a common set of best practices in creating and implementing a successful eBusiness strategy. This section of the book presents a five-step methodology for executives to use in assessing the current state of their organization and to devise an eBusiness strategy that will produce a significant impact—in quantifiable terms such as increased revenues, productivity, and customer satisfaction—in a reasonable amount of time. The results will differ, of course, for each organization, but the experience of our customers provides a basis for comparison: On average, organizations that implemented our eBusiness applications realized a return on investment within ten months after deploying the technology and reported average increases of 20 percent in productivity, 21 percent in customer satisfaction, and 15 percent in revenue.

Before turning to the step-by-step methodology, managers should keep in mind three general principles to guide the process:

- Maintain a bias for action.
- Prototype rapidly, test, and adjust.
- Leverage investments in legacy systems.

Maintain a Bias for Action

While the methodology presented below involves varying degrees of analysis at specific points, speed is a critical factor in eBusiness success—especially in situations where there is substantial risk that competitors may gain pre-emptive advantages by implementing their eBusiness capabilities first. In today's world, that threat looms large for virtually every organization.

Therefore, in devising and implementing an eBusiness strategy, organizations must strike a balance between thorough analysis and rapid action, with a bias toward launching quickly. It is easy to become mired in analysis, but the accelerating pace of today's business climate demands that organizations move swiftly. Managers, therefore, must adjust their mind-sets and gear their organizations to favor action over inertia—a key component of an eBusiness-oriented organizational culture. In the past, organizations had the luxury of devoting far more time to studying and evaluating options. Today, however, with product life cycles growing shorter and shorter and with competition rising from all directions, organizations cannot afford to delay taking action.

Prototype Rapidly, Test, and Adjust

The imperative to move swiftly also means that the organization need not precisely plot every aspect of the strategy before acting. While the methodology presented here calls for devising several plans—for example, a plan to address organizational change requirements—organizations can confidently launch their eBusiness strategy without working out the full details of each plan in advance. The experience of eBusiness pioneers shows that a significant number of the assumptions incorporated in highly detailed plans turn out to be totally inaccurate, with valuable time and resources wasted on trying to capture too much detail. Therefore, the optimal approach to eBusiness planning and implementation is to prototype the model rapidly, test it, measure the results, and adjust according to those results. By incorporating appropriate prototyping and test phases into the implementation, organizations can mitigate the risk of acting quickly and on limited analysis.

Leverage Investments in Legacy Systems

Transforming an organization into an eBusiness overnight is not feasible. Organizations must build eBusiness capabilities in phases, initially concentrating on their greatest "points of pain" or on the area of greatest potential return. But no matter where organizations direct their initial eBusiness efforts, they do not need to scrap their existing information technology infrastructure and start over. Many organizations have invested enormous resources over long periods in their current systems, which house valuable data and perform critical functions. In most cases, organizations can leverage prior investments by integrating their eBusiness architecture with these legacy systems, then building on top of the new architecture to extend the functionality of the overall system. With this approach, the organization develops its eBusiness capabilities through tightly focused efforts that produce significant but incremental wins.

Country Companies Insurance Group, for example, a U.S. insurer that provides life, health, property, and automobile policies, had invested almost thirty years in its back-office mainframe systems. The legacy systems run applications that handle billing, underwriting, and record maintenance, and they also house multiple customer databases for Country Companies' various insurance lines. The company needed to leverage this vital data so that sales and service agents could get up-to-date views of each customer to more effectively serve customers and cross-sell products. Rather than abandon its legacy systems, Country Companies came to us to implement an eBusiness application—Siebel *e*Insurance—tailored specifically for the insurance industry, in order to standardize the information available to its field agents, call center service representatives, and other customer-facing personnel. Country Companies is rolling out the new system in phases to three call centers, two marketing divisions, a customer acquisition center, and corporate headquarters. More than 3,000 employees will ultimately use the system, and Country Companies will eventually extend the system to the Internet, providing customers with Web-based self-service. By implementing a common, scalable platform to handle customer information, Country Companies now has a foundation to easily extend eBusiness capabilities across all channels, all lines of business, and all functional areas of the organization.

The Five-Step Methodology

The following methodology involves five major steps:

1. Analyze the current situation to develop an eBusiness vision and prescription.
2. Design the multichannel strategy required to fulfill the prescription.
3. Develop specific action plans for executing the strategy.
4. Implement and deploy the eBusiness system.
5. Measure, monitor, and track the eBusiness strategy.

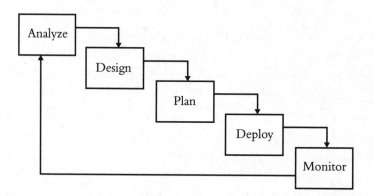

Five-step methodology for devising and implementing an eBusiness strategy

As the diagram above suggests, the process of developing an eBusiness strategy is ongoing: the organization continuously monitors the results of implementing the strategy, and these results then become inputs into the next iteration of the strategy. Each organization will have to adapt these steps to its unique circumstances.

Effective development of an eBusiness strategy requires many skills, but above all else it requires uncompromising honesty and objectivity. Organizations, like individuals, often demonstrate strong biases that can lead to suboptimal and counterproductive results. In conducting the "How to Become an eBusiness" methodology outlined here, organizations must ask penetrating questions, and they must demand valid evidence for every significant assumption or claim that they make.

In the end, successful strategy and action can come only from a rigorous analysis of the environment and a brutally honest examination of the organization. Given the natural tendency toward self-delusion and distorted perception, organizations may benefit from the use of skilled independent facilitators to lead them through this process.

CHAPTER EIGHTEEN

Analyze:
The eBusiness Readiness Assessment

The eBusiness Readiness Assessment is a preliminary process by which the organization

- diagnoses its current situation
- develops a vision of what it needs to achieve
- defines a high-level "prescription for eBusiness"

Having defined its eBusiness prescription, the organization can then proceed to the next steps, which involve designing and executing specific action plans required to achieve the objectives.

Diagnose the Current Situation

The objective of the diagnosis is to identify the organization's eBusiness potential and to begin to understand, from a high-level strategic perspective, where eBusiness initiatives will have the most significant impact or quickest return. In some cases, the starting point for the eBusiness transformation will be obvious; in other cases, figuring out where to begin the transformation will take hard-headed analysis.

For many organizations, the diagnosis is a matter of pinpointing a specific source of pain—for example, an unacceptably low rate of customer retention due to suboptimal service processes and capabilities—to which an eBusiness solution can be applied. That initial solution would then serve as the foundation for other eBusiness initiatives, with the organization learning from and building on that experience to extend its eBusiness capabilities in other directions. At online postage vendor Stamps.com, for example, the initial point of pain was the challenge of handling a much larger volume and scope of customer service inquiries than had been anticipated, which drove the company's decision to implement an eBusiness solution based on our call center software. The success of that deployment grew into a much broader application of integrated service and sales functionality, across both the Web and the call center. As a result, the new system is developing into a standardized platform used by all of the company's employees in managing customer relationships.

For other organizations, the diagnosis might point toward developing eBusiness capabilities to take advantage of as-yet-unrealized market opportunities. For example, The Sharper Image's decision to deploy our eAuction software was driven by its desire to extend its business model by adding online auction capability—a capability that the company correctly thought would provide a new source of revenue.

The diagnosis begins by analyzing the organization's current state, both internally and externally. At this stage, the analysis is very high-level and broad, attempting to capture the "big picture." To conduct the diagnosis, the organization must assign an eBusiness strategy team that will audit the organization's existing plans and strategy and will interview senior executives, channel and strategic partners, key customers, and other key constituents and stakeholders. Unless the organization has the internal expertise, resources, and objective viewpoint to perform the analysis, the team will greatly benefit from working with experienced independent consultants to direct the diagnosis.

The diagnosis focuses on operations at the corporate and business-unit levels (or the equivalent levels in public-sector organizations). The diagnosis assesses the organization's existing eBusiness capabilities and identifies, at a macro level, gaps between expected and actual performance.

The internal data inputs come from a variety of sources—such as interviews with executives, middle managers, and frontline supervisors; strategy and planning documents; and observation—and they include:

- Business plan (business conditions and financials; products; markets; channels)
- Growth strategy (how does the organization plan to grow?)
- Current multichannel strategy (what channels is the organization using?)
- Strategy deployment (how is the organization executing current strategy?)
- Defined achievements and barriers of organization's current strategy deployment
- High-level description of organization's human resources, key business processes, and information technology infrastructure
- Statement of the organization's key performance expectations (e.g., growth, profitability, market share, customer satisfaction)
- eBusiness vision (what are the organization's preliminary ideas about its eBusiness goals?)
- Description of desired future state: in what key aspects does the organization wish that its future state look significantly different from its current state? (e.g., a product-centric organization wants to become a customer-centric organization)
- eBusiness strengths and weaknesses assessment

Externally, the diagnosis consists of an "environmental scan," which captures key aspects of the industry: customer segments, the organization's market share (and its market share expectations), and so on. The environmental scan also surveys the competitive landscape within the industry, determining which established competitors occupy which positions and identifying key sources of potential new competition, as well as "holes" in the market where various customer segments are being underserved.

Assessing eBusiness Strengths and Weaknesses

A key component of the diagnosis is to assess the organization's eBusiness strengths and weaknesses: the eBusiness strategy team should score the organization's capabilities against each of the eight eBusiness principles described in Part II. This helps to identify major gaps between the organization's current and ideal states of eBusiness readiness. How well or how effectively does the organization:

1. know its customers?
2. use multiple channels to interact with its customers?
3. personalize the customer experience?
4. optimize the lifetime value of every customer? (Does the organization even have a process in place to determine the lifetime value of customers?)
5. focus on 100 percent customer satisfaction?
6. deploy a global, customer-centric eBusiness architecture?
7. leverage and extend its eBusiness ecosystem?
8. cultivate a culture built on eBusiness excellence and innovation?

Answering these questions requires the organization to conduct a probing introspection. For example, in assessing how well it knows its customers, an organization must specify, among other things, exactly what categories of customer information it regularly records and tracks; what processes it uses to capture this information; and how that information is analyzed and leveraged to achieve specific marketing, sales, and service goals. For each of the eight principles, the organization must ask similarly searching questions that are relevant to its specific industry and marketplace. Through this analysis, the organization can begin to develop a preliminary sense of priorities relating to potential eBusiness efforts and investments.

Growth Strategy Analysis

Another key aspect of the diagnosis is to evaluate the organization's growth strategy: how does the organization plan to grow its business—that is, which combinations of products and markets are expected to drive the organization's growth? An organization's rate of growth is the single most important factor determining shareholder value, and every organization today is under increasing pressure from shareholders to grow at unprecedented rates. Therefore, no matter what its growth objectives or expectations, every organization must have a deliberate strategy for deriving its targeted revenues.

One way to analyze growth strategy is to use a simple model that involves just two considerations: which products and services (existing or new?) will be sold; and to which customers (existing or new?) will they be sold. Modeled as a 2x2 matrix, the cells of the matrix represent each of the four possible combinations:

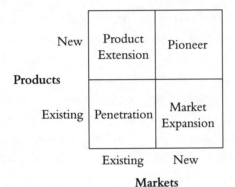

1. Sell existing products to existing customers (penetration).
2. Sell existing products to new customers (market expansion).
3. Sell new products to existing customers (product extension).
4. Sell new products to new customers (pioneer).

Based on this simple model, the organization should determine what portion of planned revenues will come from which of the four possible strategies. This is important, because each strategy requires a different combination of capabilities; a different go-to-market approach (including different marketing tactics, sales structures and channels, and postsale service programs); and a different allocation of resources (i.e., varying levels of expertise and cost in sales, marketing, and service). The organization's major objective, therefore, is to identify the potential market segments that it proposes to serve in order to reach its revenue goals.

In particular, the team must analyze the market dynamics for each potential market segment identified in the growth-strategy analysis, in order to validate and prioritize them. This step requires examining several key factors for each segment:

Size. What is the current total volume of business in this segment? What is the projected growth?

Competitive landscape. Who are the competitors in these segments, what are their positions and shares, and what are the strengths and weaknesses of each? How consolidated or fragmented is this market: is the trend toward more fragmentation (many new entrants) or greater consolidation?

Market value chain. How is value created and delivered to customers in this market? How much relative power does each link of the market value chain have? (In apparel, for example, large manufacturers such as Levi Strauss have considerable power over their suppliers, but large retailers such as Sears in turn have considerable power over manufacturers.)

Customer dynamics. Who are the customers in this segment? What are their key characteristics? What product and service attributes do they most value? What drives demand? What is the purchase decision and buying process?

Reachability. How are customers reached? What are the dominant channels, and what volume of total market business goes through each channel? Who actually touches the customer (e.g., do producers sell direct, or are there intermediary distribution layers)?

Evaluate the Organization's Capabilities and Prioritize the Gaps

By analyzing the market dynamics of each targeted segment, as outlined in the previous step, the organization develops an understanding of what is required to effectively serve each segment. The next step is to evaluate the organization's capabilities against these requirements. This evaluation serves two purposes: one, it identifies the gaps between existing capabilities and requirements; and, two, it stimulates ideas for filling those gaps. The evaluation focuses on four categories of an organization's capabilities: products, services, expertise, and technology.

Products. The organization must assess the match between its products and the preferences of the market segments it intends to serve. In every market, for instance, products have to deliver a minimum threshold of characteristics (certain minimal features, quality, reliability, etc.). Products that do not meet these basic requirements quickly fail. Beyond these basics, however, the more penetrating question is: How well do the products excel on the various dimensions that are most highly valued by customers in the target segments?

Services. Every offering, whether tangible or intangible, incorporates a service component. The organization must therefore assess whether its existing service capabilities meet the requirements of the market segments it is targeting. Suppose, for example, that a high-end computer maker has decided to grow its business by targeting the segment of low-end PC buyers. This strategy obviously has implications for the firm's product and channel capabilities, but it also affects the company's service capabilities: low-end, novice users ask different kinds of questions than do sophisticated high-end users, and have a different value perspective about service. Therefore, the company may need to create a new service capability for the low-end segment, in addition to configuring the product for novice users.

Expertise. Expertise includes specialized skills, distinct business processes, unique knowledge, and other elements that together constitute the organization's core competencies. The organization must ask, Do we have all of the expertise required to serve the market segments that we are targeting? If not, where are the gaps, and what are the options for closing those gaps? Levi Strauss, for example, discontinued selling merchandise directly to consumers over the Internet, because it concluded it did not have the retail expertise to profitably do so; in contrast, retail partners Macy's and

JCPenney have extensive expertise in this area. This realization is driving Levi's new online strategy, with implications for how its Web activities must integrate with those of its retail partners.

Technology. Technology includes information systems, fulfillment and distribution systems, and manufacturing and production systems. An eBusiness strategy can have implications for any or all of these technology capabilities.

In order for the organization to execute its chosen eBusiness strategy, some gaps will be more critical to close than others. The organization, therefore, must assess the relative importance of each gap to the success of its strategy. For those gaps with high priority, the organization must develop plans for eliminating the gap. Possible solutions might include, for instance, making an acquisition to gain a missing capability, partnering to fill in a gap, or investing in a new channel. Recently, for example, BT Wholesale Services and Solutions, a unit of British telecommunications giant BT, concluded that it needed to add the Web as a new channel. As a result of the unit's aggressive strategy to roll out high-speed DSL service throughout the United Kingdom, BT Wholesale expected to experience a sixfold increase in orders—from about 360,000 annually to more than 2 million—over the next two years. BT Wholesale determined that its existing fax-based ordering system could not scale to serve such a surge in demand. The unit therefore developed an eBusiness solution called e.Co Order based on our eBusiness applications, which integrates its sales, service, and marketing infrastructure into a single, comprehensive, multichannel system. Extending the management of customer relationships beyond fax and telephone contact, e.Co Order enables customers to interact with the company through whichever channel they choose—via the Web, telephone, fax, or in person.

Develop the eBusiness Vision

The high-level diagnosis just completed enables the organization to sense where the application of an eBusiness strategy will have a significant impact. Now the focus shifts to developing a more articulated vision of eBusiness possibilities. To develop this vision, the team must assess and profile several key aspects of the organization:

- What are the current strategies and expectations?
- What are the most significant business challenges?
- What is the level of executive commitment to eBusiness?
- What are the potential barriers, as well as key success factors, to executing an eBusiness strategy?
- What are the organization's long-term performance objectives, and where are the gaps between the current state and the desired future state?

Wrestling with and resolving those questions yields the broad outlines of an eBusiness vision. By pinpointing the organization's most significant challenges and assessing the gaps between current performance and future objectives, this vision provides a strategic view of where the organization's eBusiness strategy should be focused.

Define the eBusiness Prescription

The final step of the analysis phase is to specify an eBusiness prescription, which narrows the focus of the strategy into more specific terms that will drive detailed action plans. For a global PC manufacturer, for example, the eBusiness prescription might be stated thus: we must add an Internet channel for our business customers, enhance the presence and performance of our call center and retail channels, and reduce our direct sales force by 25 percent.

Developing the eBusiness prescription requires analysis at a finer level of detail than is involved in either the diagnosis or vision steps. For example, it entails developing key benchmarks and identifying best practices. It also requires conducting a high-level validation and feasibility study of the proposed prescription, based on rough-cut financial data, in order to determine a general estimate of the required investment. A more thorough financial analysis occurs in the next phase, when resource requirements are more finely specified.

CHAPTER NINETEEN

Design the Multichannel Strategy

The input into this phase is the eBusiness prescription that was defined in the previous phase. The objective now is to design the multichannel strategy required to achieve the goals stated in the prescription. This entails identifying the required resources and capabilities and analyzing the financial impact on the organization. At this stage, the analysis becomes more detailed. The major components are the development of "channel maps," "customer-experience maps," and a channel integration strategy.

Creating Channel Maps

A channel map details the costs and benefits—by channel, by product or service, and by market segment—of marketing, selling to, and servicing customers in the segments targeted by the organization's growth strategy. The organization conducts this channel map analysis to ensure that its multichannel strategy will return acceptable levels of revenues, profit, productivity, and customer satisfaction. Inputs into the channel map analysis include:

- channel cost data
- product/service profitability data
- customer-buying criteria, needs, and preferences
- expected benefits (revenues, exposure, market share, etc.)

The channel map shows, in detail, what customers in each targeted segment require, by channel, for every product or service that the organization markets to those customers. Channel map analysis is a powerful tool for investigating the effectiveness of both existing and proposed strategies. Channel map analysis might reveal, for example, that a direct-sales channel is losing money for the organization by serving a bottom tier of customers who are interested only in the organization's base product; and, by analyzing the actual criteria and preferences of these customers, the channel map indicates that these customers do not require personal handling by a direct sales representative—they just want to purchase the product and move on. In this case, therefore, the implication would be to serve those customers through a lower-cost channel.

The channel map also serves as the basis for developing a return on investment (ROI) model to analyze the financial impact of the proposed multichannel strategy (including any solutions to fill the gaps required to serve the targeted segment). This answers the question Will it pay? Performing this analysis requires detailed cost data by product and channel, as well as assumptions about the expected benefits of the strategy. Benefits include incremental profits and cost savings that can be expected to result from the strategy, projected over an appropriate period of time and discounted by an appropriate rate to a net present value (NPV). Organizations should test the sensitivity of their NPV calculations by varying key input factors such as expected incremental profit. If the NPV calculation is highly sensitive to a particular variable, the organization may want to refine its analysis to develop a more confident forecast of that factor under the new strategy.

Creating Customer–Experience Maps

In addition to determining that the proposed multichannel strategy meets the organization's ROI requirement, the organization must also ensure that the strategy will positively impact the customer experience. Creating the customer-experience map provides the organization with a view of what the customer is exposed to during every interaction throughout the customer life cycle and through any given channel. The map also shows what must happen in the background (i.e., not seen or directly experienced by the customer) to ensure customer satisfaction. The map reflects every process that affects the customer experience, whether or not that process is "visible" either to the customer or to the organization.

The organization creates the customer-experience map by identifying each element in the marketing, sales, and service processes, including channel partner processes. This analysis indicates each touch point that customers experience in their interactions with the organization. For example, the customer-experience map at a diversified financial services organization might indicate that a single customer who uses several of the organization's services—for example, checking account, credit card, home-equity loan—must deal with a separate service center for each one, forcing the customer to call different numbers for service on the different products. As a result, the organization may decide to integrate its service operations in order to streamline and improve the customer's experience.

Formulating a Channel Integration Strategy

Not only must each of the organization's channels—the Web, call center, field service and sales, and so on—be individually optimized, but they must all be integrated so that the customer has a consistent and satisfying experience, regardless of the channel that is chosen. In the financial-services example above, the customer-experience map indicated that the organization's service operations for the different product lines were not integrated, causing considerable inconvenience to the customer. This led the organization to conclude that it needed to integrate its service channels, so that a customer can call just one number to receive service for any of the organization's products. By analyzing its channel maps and customer-experience maps, the organization can pinpoint precisely how channel integration needs to occur in order to deliver a satisfying customer experience.

Determine Final Objectives for the eBusiness Strategy and Implementation Plan

Based on the foregoing analyses, the organization specifies the key objectives for its eBusiness strategy. In reality, the design of specific eBusiness initiatives is an iterative process, with analysis looping back as more information and considerations come to light. It will often take several passes to arrive at a strategy that is expected to produce an acceptable ROI and a significant impact on the organization's overall competitive advantage. The output of this step is a well-defined set of eBusiness objectives, including a financial model that estimates ROI, which then drives the subsequent planning processes. Objectives will typically take the form of quantifiable goals to be achieved within a certain time frame.

CHAPTER TWENTY

Develop Detailed Action Plans

The contents of an organization's detailed eBusiness action plans will, of course, depend on the organization's specific objectives determined in the previous step and on its particular circumstances. However, every implementation must address the issues of organizational change and the composition and assignment of the "virtual customer team."

Develop a Plan for Organizational Change and Change Management

"Years of study and experience," writes Harvard Business School professor Rosabeth Moss Kanter, a renowned scholar of organizational behavior, "show that the things that sustain change are not bold strokes but long marches—the independent, discretionary, ongoing efforts of people throughout the organization." Indeed, often the most challenging aspect of implementing an eBusiness strategy is to orchestrate the "long marches" required to execute the strategy. For example, focusing on 100 percent customer satisfaction introduces a new set of priorities and processes for many organizations, which require a significant shift in long-entrenched managerial mind-sets. Therefore, the organization must devise and execute a conscious plan for driving the required change throughout the entire organization—and the ultimate responsibility for ensuring that the necessary changes take hold lies with senior management.

According to change expert John P. Kotter of Harvard Business School, a primary cause of unsuccessful change efforts is management's failure to create throughout the organization a sense of urgency to change. In any major change initiative, the likelihood of resistance and complacency is high: significant change requires exceptional effort and imposes temporary discomfort that comes from learning new ways of doing things—yet the organizational tendency is toward inertia and maintaining the status quo. A key task of change agents, therefore, is to identify the sources of resistance and complacency, and to devise strategies to counter these tendencies. In other words, the change process needs to be planned and managed, which involves four major steps:

- define the organizational change objectives and requirements
- provide appropriate training
- institutionalize the change plan
- design compensation schemes that will reinforce the change objectives

Define organizational change objectives. In addition to defining its eBusiness objectives, the organization must also define the organizational change required to support and execute the eBusiness strategy. For example, if the strategy requires sales personnel to move from a paper-based system of compiling customer information to the use of a common eBusiness platform, then the organization must identify this objective and specify this expected change of behavior as a requirement for sales personnel. This change will occur more quickly and with less resistance if the sales force is initially consulted in the design and testing phases of the system implementation (see below).

Provide appropriate training. Organizational change almost always requires some degree of support in the form of training. In the example mentioned above, the organization needs to set up sufficient training resources for sales personnel, to coach them through the transition from their idiosyncratic paper-based method of managing contact information to the use of the new system. Training requirements and resources, therefore, must be explicitly part of the organizational change plan. Particularly with the rollout of new technology and systems, effective training is essential to end-user acceptance and use of the technology—a finding that our training division can confirm in providing services to clients such as Yahoo!, Rockwell, U.S. Bank, Cabletron, and Perrier.

A significant component of end-user training involves change management. In fact, at Siebel Systems, we estimate that about 40 percent of every effective, well-designed end-user training program must focus on educating course recipients about the process changes associated with the new eBusiness system—and the benefits the individuals will experience in their jobs by using the technology—while 60 percent of training involves the transfer of specific skills. Trainees must understand why they are being trained; what the desired outcomes and goals are; and how the new technology will enable them to do their jobs more effectively. Organizations should not underestimate the challenges of the change-management aspects of training: it is generally more difficult to alter the mind-set and work habits of employees than to teach them new skills. Therefore, managers must reinforce training with appropriate organizational changes—such as new compensation structures and job-evaluation policies—designed to drive the desired behavior.

Training, therefore, involves instructing personnel both on the use of new information technology and in new processes. In addressing these twin aspects of training, organizations must avoid a common pitfall associated with significant change initiatives: "One mistake many organizations make," writes Professor Jeffrey Pfeffer, a renowned scholar of organizational culture at Stanford Business School, "is to upgrade the skills of both managers and workers but not change the structure for work in ways that permit people to do anything different. Under such circumstances, it is little wonder that training has no apparent effect."[27]

For example, though eBusiness technology may provide customer service agents with extensive information about a customer's account, the organization still may not achieve significant increases in customer satisfaction unless organizational policies empower agents to take proactive measures to resolve customer inquiries—for example, permit service agents to adjust a customer's invoice up to a certain limit. (This type of automatic approval, subject to specific restrictions, can easily be programmed into an eBusiness system.) Avoiding such disconnects between training and process redesign requires that managers fully align business processes, IT requirements, and organizational policies as they devise the eBusiness strategy and system.

Institutionalize the change plan. In order to succeed, eBusiness strategy must come from the top, but it must also be supported throughout the organization. Ideally, the strategy-development process will have involved the key people whose "buy-in" is necessary for the strategy to succeed, and they already will be committed champions of the plan. In any case, it is the change leader's responsibility to secure the commitment of those who must actually drive change throughout various parts of the organization. In essence, this is the job of creating a burning "sense of urgency" that rallies the organization behind the eBusiness strategy.

Senior executives who are charged with this task can take several actions:

- Solicit the involvement and input of key personnel early in the strategy-development process, to instill among these people a sense of ownership, importance, and personal pride in the success of the organization's eBusiness strategy.
- Investigate the best practices across their industry. Executives can accelerate this task by working with vendors who have proven experience in delivering high-yield eBusiness solutions and a deep understanding of the organization's industry. Such vendors include software and hardware firms, management consultants, and systems integrators.
- Lead by example: subordinates gauge the importance of an objective largely by how much time and energy their supervisors devote to it. If subordinates do not detect genuine passion for the plan among higher-ups, they are not likely to develop passion for it either.
- Communicate regularly with key members of the strategy-execution team in a two-way dialogue: require periodic progress

reports from them, but also give them frequent status reports about what is happening in other parts of the eBusiness plan. Team players are further energized by a sense of progress from the entire team.

- To reach frontline personnel, concentrate communication efforts on frontline supervisors. According to communication experts T. J. Larkin and Sandar Larkin, authors of *Communicating Change*, research shows that frontline personnel respond far more positively to change when their supervisors present the new requirements than when the edicts come from senior management. Futhermore, the best way to communicate with frontline supervisors is for individual senior managers to meet with these supervisors face-to-face, either one on one or in small groups, to explain the change program. When supervisors have bought into the new organizational requirements, they can then translate these requirements into actionable terms tailored to specific frontline roles.

Design reinforcing compensation schemes. Compensation schemes designed to reinforce organizational objectives are a powerful mechanism for motivating change. As previously noted, for instance, employees are more likely to care about customer satisfaction if a significant part of their compensation is based on high satisfaction scores. Two major challenges for organizations are: one, to balance the rewards for short-term goals against those for long-term objectives; and, two, to align compensation schemes throughout the entire organization so that all employees are working in concert toward the same goals and not at cross-purposes. This could happen, for example, if senior managers are primarily being rewarded on quarterly profit results while line personnel are rewarded primarily on customer satisfaction scores.

Develop the Multichannel "Virtual Customer Team"

A major effect of eBusiness on organizations is the breaking down of rigid divides between departments, functions, and other unit structures.

As eBusiness enables—in fact, requires—the free flow of information across channels and throughout the entire ecosystem, the organization must develop a similar fluidity in how it interacts with customers. For most organizations, this means a far greater degree of cross-functional processes than they have deployed in the past.

In addition, the complexity, pace, and global scope of today's business environment requires organizations to tightly integrate their customer-facing processes with those of their channel partners. Organizations must be able to manage channel partners as virtual extensions of their marketing, sales, and service operations. This means, for example, coordinating customer interactions with channel partners, so that customers receive consistent, unified messaging and enjoy a seamless experience. Consider a typical scenario in which a manufacturer uses marketing programs to generate leads for its channel partners. In all too many of such programs, the handoff of leads to channel partners does not function smoothly: leads are lost or misrouted, or there are long delays in following up on leads. As a result, everyone loses: the potential customer is annoyed by the lack of response (and has probably gone to the competition), and both the channel partner and manufacturer have lost an opportunity. This broken process can be fixed by applying an eBusiness solution: an integrated system that directly connects the manufacturer's lead-generation program with its channel partners, thereby providing all parties with a comprehensive view of the same real-time information about lead activity and status.

As the organization designs its customer-touching processes, it must ensure that customers are handled in a way that produces maximum value for the organization while simultaneously promoting 100 percent customer satisfaction. The purpose of assigning the virtual customer team is to define the roles and responsibilities of all team members to achieve the twin goals of maximum customer value and 100 percent customer satisfaction.

In the past, organizations developed various ways of assigning roles and responsibilities for members engaged in customer-facing processes. In sales, for example, this was thought of as "territory assignment"—and, as the term implied, it was typically based on matching the geography of customers with the geography of salespeople. Though this territory-based approach serves the convenience of the organization, it does not leverage customer information to take into account important customer characteristics, nor does it make optimal use of resources.

Understand your customer. Like every key aspect of eBusiness, developing the virtual customer team begins with precise knowledge of the customer, which drives the specific composition of the team and the definition of roles and responsibilities. For example, the virtual team assigned to key strategic accounts will not be the same as that assigned to small business customers. The team for a strategic account, for instance, will likely include a dedicated account manager, with specialized expertise relevant to the account's industry, who has developed a tight relationship with contacts within the account. Other team members might include specific support personnel at the customer contact center: when a call from the strategic account comes into the center, the eBusiness system recognizes it as such and routes the call to one of the designated team members who have the specialized knowledge and skills to handle inquiries from that account.

Coordinating the activities of global teams spread across multiple geographies is an especially challenging problem for many organizations. At WorldCom's Global Markets division, for example, sales teams sell into the largest organizations in the world, and some teams, focused on a single account, can be as large as thirty people. To enable teams to share data around the world, the WorldCom unit employs eBusiness software that is used by some 3,000 field personnel. Another customer of ours— a leading producer of smart-card solutions—has extensive operations across multiple continents. Because much of the company's sales effort is targeted toward complex negotiations with telecommunications companies, teamwork is instrumental to the company's success. By using eBusiness applications to integrate its sales operations, the company more easily gathers together its international sales teams in support of complex sales proposals. It uses the software to create a single, comprehensive view of each customer and to ensure consistent analysis and interpretation of information. In addition, the system is helping to break down the cultural barriers within the company's global sales organization—for the first time giving the company the ability to analyze sales information from its Chinese, Russian, Latin American, and European operations in a standardized format, irrespective of cultural differences.

Organize resources around the customer. Organizations typically design processes and structures from a product-centric perspective. Financial-services institutions, for example, create separate business units for depository accounts (checking and savings), credit cards, mortgages, investment accounts, trusts, and so on. While that approach might make sense from the organization's perspective, it generally is a barrier to providing a seamless customer experience. The customer who has a checking account, credit card, and mortgage with the same institution views that institution as an organic whole and wants to interact with it as a single entity. Therefore, the organization must align virtual team resources by customer rather than by product, while harnessing the deep product knowledge of experts as needed.

Assign the integrated, virtual team. The virtual team is the collection of marketing, sales, and service personnel, supported by associated channel resources, that will actually engage the customer at any specific touch point. At Chase Manhattan Bank, for example, retail customers are segmented by assets and level of activity with the bank, and the customer team assignments are based on those classifications. Customers who carry a certain minimum balance, for instance, are designated as "Select Banking" customers and are assigned a dedicated Relationship Manager to handle all of their banking needs.

Define roles and responsibilities of team members. A multichannel eBusiness strategy means that marketing, sales, and service resources will be allocated based on relevant customer characteristics. Each team member must have a clearly assigned role and responsibility. At Dell, for example, the field sales force has the primary role of acquiring new accounts, but once an account is acquired the telesales and Web channels pick up the process and are assigned to retain that customer. While the sales force continues to work with established customers on complex purchases, part of the sales force's responsibility is to educate and condition new customers to use the call center or Web for all of their routine transactions.

Optimize virtual team incentives based on key objectives such as profitability, retention, and customer satisfaction. Every organization has to balance the requirements of developing new business against the requirements of retaining existing business. In addition, the organization's objective is to acquire and retain profitable customers who will remain loyal to the organization over time. Therefore, compensation and incentives for the virtual team members must be structured to reinforce all of these objectives—new business development, profitability, and customer satisfaction and loyalty—in a balanced way. For instance, payment of the full sales commission on a new account might be conditioned on that account remaining a customer for some specified period.

CHAPTER TWENTY-ONE

Implement and Deploy
the eBusiness System

Implementing and deploying the eBusiness system comes only after the critical work of strategic analysis has been done and concrete eBusiness objectives have been defined. This way, the system can be designed to serve strategic goals rather than the other way around. Two key factors to a successful implementation are: follow a structured process; and adopt a rapid-deployment approach.

Follow a Structured Process

Organizations can structure the eBusiness implementation in six stages:

1. Project definition. During this stage, the organization develops and assigns the project team; finalizes the project scope and approach; and determines and implements the project management control features (such as milestones, reporting requirements, and documentation requirements).

2. Discovery. During this stage, the project team gathers the functional and technical requirements that are needed to support the eBusiness objectives. Team members observe processes, interview functional managers, and analyze data in order to refine and document the requirements that will drive the next stage: design. At this stage, and at the design and configuration stages as well, team members must pay special attention not only to technical requirements but also to process and end-user requirements. Many unsuccessful implementations result from insufficient attention to the needs and preferences of end users (whether employees, customers, or partners). End-user training requirements should be included in the discovery stage.

3. Design. In the design stage, the project team creates a mock-up of the solution. Using application screen flows and design layouts, the team maps and documents the requirements that were gathered during the discovery stage.

4. Configuration. The project team then translates the design into functioning software by configuring the application and the extensions and external interfaces required to support the new system.

5. Validation. In the validation stage, the project team performs a full-function test of the system, including an end-user acceptance test using production data.

6. Deployment. Deployment happens in two stages—the production pilot and rollout—with iterative adjustments during the production pilot before final rollout. During the pilot, the project team field-tests and revises all aspects of the new system—end-user training, technical infrastructure, the network, and the helpdesk—before deployment to the entire organization. After making the necessary revisions, the team rolls out the system to all users (using a phased rollout schedule if there are many users and multiple locations).

Adopt a Rapid-Deployment Approach

Successful eBusiness implementations are generally executed in a reasonable length of time—four to five months or so. The experience of many organizations suggests that an implementation that takes longer than four or five months is likely to be troubled. An organization can take several measures to accelerate the implementation.

Identify tractable phases. Employing a phased approach allows organizations to gain and build on quick "wins." The idea is first to fully define the overall scope of the project, based on the organization's strategic eBusiness objectives (as determined through the eBusiness assessment), then break the project down into tractable phases, each of which can be implemented in a reasonable length of time. This approach has multiple benefits. It enables end users to learn the new system more efficiently in smaller increments, which yields productivity gains more quickly. It also allows the organization more time to understand and assess future requirements, to make changes more easily during the implementation process, and to minimize surprises and isolate potential difficulties before they become problems.

Execute in parallel. Members of the eBusiness project team can carry out various pieces of the overall implementation in parallel. For example, in the early part of the implementation, different team members can simultaneously gather business requirements from different parts of the organization. In addition, as some team members begin to roll out the first phase of the overall eBusiness initiative, other members can begin work on the next phase. This way, the team leverages work and experience from prior phases.

Avoid overconfiguring the system. A common cause of a lengthy implementation is that the scope of the project has expanded too broadly, requiring the system to be "overconfigured"—that is, the project team is trying to build more functionality into the system than is optimal for the current phase. During the design phase, the project team must be on guard against "feature creep," which is the tendency for designers to keep adding functionality to the system. In some cases, the team may have to go back and negotiate with area managers to identify nonessential functions that can be temporarily excluded. This may be particularly necessary in the early eBusiness phases, when rapid deployment is often more important than full configuration.

Critical Factors for eBusiness Implementation Success

Siebel Systems has participated in more than 1,500 implementations of eBusiness solutions throughout the world, involving a broad range of industries and organizations of all sizes. Based on our extensive experience, we have observed seven factors critical to success:

1. Align the business and information technology organizations. The implementation team's structure must support the business structure and processes. In other words, the organization's business objectives must drive the requirements and design of the eBusiness solution, not the other way around—which means that the goals and vision of the IT owners of the implementation must align with those of the business owners. Misalignment can result in technology that does not adequately solve the organization's business problems or, worse, that introduces additional problems—thereby producing delays, cost overruns, employee frustration, and unhappy customers.

2. Ensure executive sponsorship. Management commitment is key to a project's success. The executive sponsor helps keep a project on time by providing resources and resolving issues in a timely manner. For example, the project sponsor meets with key staff to review project risks, issues reports on a regular basis, identifies mitigating strategies and actions, and assigns action items. The project sponsor forms a steering committee, composed of key project stakeholders and the project team, in order to identify and resolve project issues from a business-management perspective and to review and approve critical changes to the project that affect the schedule or the functionality of the solution.

3. Provide a clear definition of the business benefits. Clearly defined business benefits focus the project on the objectives of the organization and minimize changes in scope. The project team identifies benefits—such as increased revenue, productivity, and customer satisfaction—for each major requirement of the project.

4. Leverage the functionality of the eBusiness technology. The organization realizes significant benefits by relying as much as possible on the out-of-the-box capabilities built into the eBusiness applications being deployed. Minimizing the degree of customization results in lower costs, faster deployment, and less complexity in the system, which helps reduce demands on training, technical support, and administrative services.

5. Actively involve end users. The system must meet the business requirements of users if they are to take advantage of new functionality. Therefore, users must play a key part in the implementation, from providing input during the collection of requirements to the design and testing of both the system and training. Each functional area should designate end-user representatives to participate in the definition of business requirements and to approve the business design. During development, end users should also participate in user labs to verify that the system meets their needs, and they should play a central role in end-user acceptance testing and in the production pilot. The involvement of end users provides the reality checks required to implement an effective, results-oriented eBusiness solution.

6. Employ a phased implementation approach. A phased implementation approach provides the following benefits:

- End users experience the benefits of the project as early as possible.
- The project team can include feedback from users in the complete solution.
- The project sponsor realizes a return on investment incrementally, thereby increasing the probability of project success and continuation.

7. Clearly define the end-user training strategy. End users often resist change. A clear training strategy addresses their concerns in a proactive manner. A comprehensive training program must satisfy the needs of both managers and users. In addition to imparting the necessary technical skills, effective training must also demonstrate how the system meets managers' and end users' business needs. Moreover, end-user education should begin even before users enter a formal instructional program, by communicating with the end-user community throughout all phases of the implementation. Two effective communication tactics include:

- The use of regular "town meetings" to keep end users up to date on the progress of the project and the features of the solution.
- A regular newsletter to describe the benefits of the project to the organization, the schedule, and the project's progress.

By following these cross-industry best practices, an organization significantly increases its likelihood of realizing a smooth and rapid eBusiness implementation.

CHAPTER TWENTY-TWO

Monitor, Measure, and Track: The eBusiness Scorecard

The only way to know if the organization's eBusiness strategy is working is to closely monitor, measure, and track its performance. To do this, the organization must determine which factors to measure, devise the procedures by which they are to be measured, and develop a reporting process that distributes the information to the necessary parties.

One tool for organizing this process is the "eBusiness Scorecard," a concept based on the widely used "balanced scorecard" device, which is used to link an organization's actions to its strategy. The balanced scorecard—an idea refined by Harvard Business School professor Robert Kaplan and consultant David Norton, authors of *The Balanced Scorecard*—seeks to provide organizations with a "strategic feedback system to test, validate, and modify the hypotheses embedded in a business–unit strategy." The central idea is to translate strategic objectives into a list of concrete "outcome measures," which are linked to their "performance drivers" via a sequence of assumed cause-and-effect relationships.

If, for example, increased customer retention is an important strategic objective, then the organization must determine what are the performance drivers of customer loyalty—that is, what actions can the organization take that will increase customer retention—and then construct standards to measure those actions. For instance, analysis might indicate that faster order-to-delivery time is a key driver of improved customer retention, and this may be a variable that the organization will measure. Initially, managers may have no research to validate their hypothesized cause–effect relationships; so one purpose of the monitoring system will be to test these hypotheses, which may need to be revised or refined as measurement data come in.

A second key aspect of the balanced scorecard concept is that outcomes should be measured from multiple perspectives. Kaplan and Norton prescribe four such perspectives: financial, customer, internal-business processes, and learning and growth. How many variables should the organization measure? There is no preset number. The organization should measure as many as are critical to achieving the organization's objectives. Just as a pilot would not fly a jet plane using a single instrument, Kaplan and Norton point out in their book, neither should managers try to execute a strategy using too few controls.

Proactively Seek Customer Feedback

In the era of eBusiness, one variable that every organization should measure, via one metric or another, is customer satisfaction. To do this effectively, the organization must proactively seek customer feedback, explicitly asking customers to grade the organization's performance. Methodologies for tracking customer satisfaction vary, but the basic approach follows four main steps:

1. Identify the key customer satisfaction criteria for each relevant customer segment.
2. Survey a valid sample of customers to provide a score for each satisfaction criterion.
3. Survey a valid sample of noncustomers (i.e., competitors' customers) in the relevant segment to provide scores on each criterion, in order to determine industry benchmarks.
4. Compare the organization's scores with the industry benchmarks to identify gaps.

In monitoring and tracking customer satisfaction, it is critical to distinguish between degrees of satisfaction; most important, the organization must know what portion of its customers are "completely satisfied" rather than merely "satisfied." As noted earlier, the difference between these two responses is profound. At Allstate, for example, while 93 percent of its completely satisfied customers renew their insurance policies, only 78 percent of its satisfied customers do so.

Organizations should consider using an independent service to conduct customer satisfaction studies, for four primary reasons. First, independent providers that specialize in these services have developed skills for conducting customer surveys. Second, customers may not be as honest and direct with representatives of the organization as they will be with an independent survey outfit with which they have no relationship. Third, an independent organization may have access to very large customer databases for the entire industry, which it can use to measure and monitor industry benchmarks. And fourth, customer satisfaction data have more credibility if they come from an independent provider rather than from the organization's own surveys. This is important if the organization intends to use the data for marketing or public relations purposes.

Determine Relevant Outcomes to Measure As Well As the Standards by Which to Measure Them

For each area to be monitored, the organization must determine both the outcomes it needs to measure and the metrics (that is, standards of measurement) to employ. For some outcomes, the metrics are self-evident, while others may require ingenuity and analysis to figure out.

Design System to Monitor Target Variables

In the case of measuring customer satisfaction, for example, the monitoring system might be to contract a third party to survey customers using the methodology described above. Other variables, such as internal process outcomes, might be measured using an automated procedure that the eBusiness system is programmed to perform at predefined periods. For example, the organization may set as an objective the reduction in the time that callers wait to speak to an agent at the customer service center. The eBusiness system can be programmed to monitor callers' wait time and track this statistic as it relates to other factors involving call center performance.

Create Effective Reporting Mechanisms

The final piece of the monitoring process is to ensure that the outcome measures are reported to the relevant personnel, including appropriate frontline employees as well as managers. Using capabilities built into the eBusiness system, a reporting function can also be programmed into the automated monitoring system where appropriate. For instance, in the case of the caller-waiting statistic mentioned above, the system can be further programmed to compile a report and e-mail it to a predefined list of recipients at designated intervals.

The reporting function closes the "feedback loop"—an essential feature of learning organizations—thereby enabling managers and frontline personnel to keep close watch on key outcome measures and to make adjustments as necessary. Further, the feedback loop provides executive management with data that will inform the next iteration of the eBusiness strategy: as the strategy evolves, the inputs from the self-monitoring eBusiness system become richer and, through cumulative experience, more tightly focused on key variables. This ability to carefully measure how well it is satisfying its customers—and to link those measurements to specific actions and processes—gives the organization a sustainable basis for competitive advantage, one that is very difficult for competitors to duplicate.

Nationwide Insurance:
Getting Closer to Its Customers

The Web is really opening up different ways of doing business for us, but we don't believe that we no longer need agents—quite the contrary. We believe that more people will be interested in getting the consultation of agents as a result of the information that they see on the Nationwide Web site.

—GEORGE MCKINNON, VICE PRESIDENT AND
CHIEF INFORMATION OFFICER, NATIONWIDE INSURANCE

NATIONWIDE INSURANCE AT A GLANCE

Founded in 1925 and based in Columbus, Ohio, Nationwide Insurance is the fourth-largest automobile insurer and fifth-largest homeowner's insurer in the United States. Through 4,200 exclusive agencies, the company offers life insurance, health insurance, retirement savings, and asset-management services. Nationwide currently handles 13 million active policies and has $115 billion in assets. The company employs 35,000 people in 37 countries around the world.

In the mid to late 1990s, Nationwide Insurance faced an increasingly competitive market, thanks in large part to the Internet. Increasing numbers of consumers were using the Web to research policy rates, service accounts, and communicate with agents. The Web had also developed into an important medium for companies and their agents to conduct online commerce and deliver one-to-one marketing messages to their customers. Several Internet-based insurance companies had emerged that were focused exclusively on the direct-to-consumer insurance busi-

ness. It was becoming apparent that the Web was fundamentally changing the business paradigm in the insurance industry and that a full uti-
lization of this new channel would become necessary for survival.

In addition, globalization and consolidation were amplifying competition in the insurance and financial-service industries. Nationwide
increasingly found itself competing against larger organizations that
offered insurance as part of a broader product offering.

Developing an eBusiness Strategy: Customer Choice

To address increasing competition and the influence of the Internet,
Nationwide set out to develop a strategic plan to integrate the Internet
into its multichannel infrastructure of call centers and exclusive agents.
The company calls its new eBusiness strategy "Customer Choice." "Customer Choice is the ability to do business with someone anytime,
anywhere, and through any method they choose," explains George
McKinnon, Vice President and Chief Information Officer, Nationwide
Insurance. "This involves selling services to our customers through a variety of access points, including agents and the Internet, and servicing them
through these same channels depending on the customer's preference. "

The roots of Customer Choice extend back to 1996, the year
Nationwide deployed an eBusiness field sales application to more than
2,500 users throughout the United States. With this deployment,
Nationwide began the process of consolidating its customer data into a
central repository. Previously, the vast amount of customer information
stored in Nationwide's databases was maintained in virtual silos, often
segmented by type of policy or service. As a result, the company was
missing opportunities to cross-sell services, deliver personalized marketing campaigns, and deliver the best possible customer service. Nationwide's agents were unable to utilize information derived from the sale of
one type of service to sell customers on other services. Moreover, the
lack of complete electronic profiles of customers meant that Nationwide
had to rely heavily on its agents to manually service the needs of its
customers—from answering billing questions to processing claims to
reviewing expanded coverage.

With the deployment of the eBusiness system, agents were able to access a customer's complete profile—across product lines—on their desktops or via their mobile computing devices while on the road. Having this comprehensive view of customers enabled agents to spend more time delivering personalized attention to customers and less time on basic administrative tasks. McKinnon emphasizes that giving customers personal attention drives loyalty in the insurance business, and that loyalty and retention are critical to success: "Retention is very important to all insurance providers, because customer acquisition costs are significant, and it's necessary to hold on to a customer for several years before that customer usually generates a profit for the provider."

Nationwide later extended the deployment of its eBusiness system to its call centers. Call center agents were able to use the applications to provide policy quotes to customers calling 1-800-NATIONWIDE. After giving a quote, service agents send out policy information to customers, and when the customers sign the contracts and send them back, they are assigned a Nationwide agent to manage the account.

The launch of Customer Choice integrates the Web into the company's multichannel system and gives consumers the ability to secure fast online quotes, service their accounts, and even make claims and purchase policies directly over the Web. McKinnon expects the development of the company's Internet channel will enhance the rest of the business. "The Web is really opening up different ways of doing business for us, but we don't believe that we no longer need agents—quite the contrary," he says. "We believe that more people will be interested in consulting with our agents as a result of the information that they see on the Nationwide Web site."

Nationwide has undertaken significant efforts to ensure seamless integration of the Internet into its business. "All of our Nationwide agents have their own Web sites that allow their customers to provide some level of service for themselves," explains McKinnon. "Rather than calling their agent, customers can go to their agent's Web site and check their bill or the status of a claim. The Web helps us enhance the capabilities of our agents to continue to outperform their competition." The agents' Web sites also allow them to generate new business even if they are not available in person.

By equipping each Web site with the exact pricing and information found through its other channels, Nationwide is able to maintain a seamless dialogue with its customers across all customer touch points. "If you ask one of our local agents for some product information, and then you go home later and decide to follow up on the Web site, you'll see the same price and information," explains McKinnon. "Then, if you have a question halfway through the online quote process, you can call up our call center and they'll be able to finish the quote for you. Finally, if you'd like, you can stop by the local agency office, and an agent will service that business for you." This level of integration enables Nationwide to display a consistent corporate presence to consumers, making them more comfortable in utilizing any of the company's channels.

Service Improves

Generally, after a customer purchases a new policy, he rarely has a reason to communicate with the provider, unless he has a question about a bill or needs to make a claim. This is why customer service is so critical to the success of insurance companies. One misstep—a caller kept on hold too long, or a delay in processing a claim—can send a customer into the arms of another provider. After all, that competitor is just a couple of mouse clicks away. Implementing its eBusiness system has allowed Nationwide to improve its customer service by providing its employees with accurate, consolidated customer data, and by automating the process by which employees answer customers' questions about their existing policies, bills, and claims.

Nationwide's eBusiness system also enables customers to access self-service features over the Internet, which has the potential to deliver significant cost savings to Nationwide. "Next to customer acquisition costs, one of the biggest costs we face are customer service costs related to answering questions about bills and processing claims," says McKinnon. "By providing customers with the ability to serve themselves over the Internet, we can realize enormous cost savings. The actual cost of interacting with a customer over the Web is just a fraction of a cent, far less than the cost of serving a customer through a call center or face-to-face." In addition, offering customers the ability to interact with Nationwide over the Web boosts customer satisfaction. "We have some customers who prefer to conduct business without human interaction," says McKinnon. "We've seen instances where customers file their own claim over the Web and then actually call their agent to thank them because they are so appreciative of the Web option."

Targeted Marketing

Another important element of Nationwide's eBusiness strategy is developing one-to-one relationships with its customers. Now that the company has a more complete understanding of its customers, it is able to analyze their profiles and purchasing and renewal habits in order to plan more targeted and personalized marketing campaigns using the Web. "The ability to do direct marketing via the Internet is extremely cost effective and the response rates we're seeing are high and quick," explains McKinnon. "We can see a low point in our call centers, then go out and do an e-mail marketing campaign, and immediately get a large number of calls and responses." McKinnon believes that those who have become accustomed to using the Web appreciate Web-based marketing efforts and the instant gratification they offer. "Buying decisions for insurance usually come up only on a semi-annual or annual cycle; therefore, the challenge is to motivate the customer to take ninety seconds to go into Nationwide.com and get a quote," says McKinnon. "In ninety seconds, that customer will be able to determine whether they're getting a good deal with their current policy. If the customer is online already, and we send an e-mail that says, 'Check this Web link out and get a quote in only ninety seconds,' the customer just might do it. It's a very powerful tool."

Optimizing Internal Operations

Implementing an eBusiness system has helped Nationwide optimize its internal operations, which has led to significant cost savings. With over 30,000 employees worldwide, many of whom travel frequently or work from home, Nationwide faces the difficult task of coordinating its employees' IT resources. By standardizing on one eBusiness platform, Nationwide is now better able to manage the distribution of software to its employees. In addition, Nationwide has improved employee productivity by making all information required to serve customers available via a single, Web-based interface.

Innovative Services

Knowing its customers better has enabled Nationwide to deliver cutting-edge insurance services. For example, the company recently used its eBusiness system and a tool called geo-mapping to quickly and accurately determine which of its customers lived in an area where a tornado had recently touched down. Agents were able to visit customers' homes before customers had even placed a call. As the company continues to expand its eBusiness system and develop closer relationships with its customers, one can expect similarly innovative programs from Nationwide in the years to come.

Nationwide management understands that it can no longer rely on its reputation and brand name alone to attract and retain customers. "The business paradigm is shifting, and we know that just being Nationwide is not enough," says McKinnon. "We need to continue to innovate and find ways to understand who our customers are and offer them the products, service, and choices that will keep them loyal Nationwide customers for life."

Quick & Reilly:
Putting Customers in Control

> It became apparent to us that customers wanted to be in control of
> how, where, and when they did business with us.
>
> —TOM QUICK, CHIEF OPERATING OFFICER, QUICK & REILLY

QUICK & REILLY AT A GLANCE

Founded in 1974, Quick & Reilly was the first New York Stock
Exchange member firm to offer discounted commissions to individuals. Since then, the firm has served more than one million clients.
With more than 2,500 employees and 118 investor centers throughout the United States, Quick & Reilly is the second-largest specialist
firm on the NYSE and one of the larger market makers on NASDAQ.
The company is now part of the FleetBoston Financial Corporation,
which is the nation's seventh-largest financial holding company, with
$179 billion in assets. FleetBoston Financial is a global financial
company, providing asset management, insurance, investment banking, and mortgage banking, as well as such retail services as checking,
savings, loans, and credit cards. The company has more than 20 million customers in more than 20 countries and territories around the
world.

In his twenty-four years with the discount brokerage firm Quick &
Reilly, Tom Quick, the company's Chief Operating Officer, has learned
a simple but important lesson: "You can't fight the customer, because he
can always go elsewhere." Therefore, when the Internet began empow-

ering consumers with information and access in the mid-1990s, Quick paid close attention. He concedes that the company was regarded at the time as a conservative company that was not very technologically advanced. "We were seen more as a traditional firm than as one of the more nimble discount firms," he says. However, Quick and his management team could see that fundamental changes in the financial services industry were imminent and that the company would need to adapt to remain an industry leader. The company therefore decided to develop an eBusiness system that would help it better meet its customers' changing needs, deliver outstanding customer service, and confront the changing dynamics of the brokerage industry.

Internet Shifts Balance of Power

Throughout the mid to late 1990s, many consumers began to use the Internet to help take control of their investments. They were becoming empowered with considerable amounts of information—including market data, professional research, and corporate financial information—and were receiving much of it in real time from Wall Street via the Web. In fact, information that had been sold for considerable amounts of money by financial advisers just a few years earlier was being made freely available to the public. Armed with newly acquired knowledge and technological savvy, consumers began to demand new ways to trade and manage their money. The Internet enabled consumers to instantly check the status of their assets, view market trends and analysis, and execute market orders. "The balance of power shifted from the broker to the customer," says Quick. "It became apparent to us that customers wanted to be in control of how, where, and when they did business with us."

Competition Intensifies

At the same time that the Internet was creating a new, highly educated type of investor, competition in the brokerage industry was intensifying. New firms and established full-service brokerage firms alike entered the discount brokerage marketplace, leading to downward price pressure.

Moreover, there emerged a rapid convergence in the financial-services industry as former independent banking, brokerage, and insurance businesses began to consolidate to offer one-stop-shop financial services. Because of the competitive pressures, Quick says that it became imperative for his firm to reexamine how it could provide value to the customer. "There is so much information out there that it can become overwhelming," says Quick. "We felt that we could differentiate Quick & Reilly by providing an integrated customer support system that would give customers the ability to move seamlessly from the Internet to the customer resource call center to a financial consultant. This system would give customers the ability to execute trades inexpensively online or through the customer resource center, but also provide them with a personal financial consultant who could assist them anytime they needed help making financial decisions or analyzing financial information."

Streamlining Business Communications

To realize its vision of a multichannel support system, Quick & Reilly needed eBusiness technology that would improve intercompany communications and enhance customer service. A number of customer requests require Quick & Reilly to interact with its clearinghouse, US Clearing. For example, when a client makes a request for funds to be transferred or checks to be mailed, the request is reviewed and sent to US Clearing to be fulfilled. It is then sent back to Quick & Reilly for verification. "The old system was paper based," says Ed Garry, Assistant Vice President of CRM Solutions, Quick & Reilly. "We were communicating with US Clearing via a wire service, which was highly inefficient and enabled only the wire sender and receiver to view the requests. Although such a system was sufficient in the traditional environment where there were never more than five or six people working with a customer, it doesn't work in a multichannel environment where there are, for example, 350 call center agents who might take a call from the customer regarding the status of the customer's account. We needed to automate our systems so that all customer-facing employees would share the same information."

Quick & Reilly also needed an eBusiness solution that would improve communication among its personal financial consultants and between its financial consultants and customers. "Once we began to look at various eBusiness solutions, we learned how access to consolidated customer information could make our financial consultants more efficient in servicing current orders, while at the same time be more productive in securing new business," says Garry. "Our financial consultants didn't have a uniform system to track events and build a calendar of activities for their day. They were left to their own devices to develop an activities management system, and there wasn't a way for financial consultants to share calendars and assign activities to each other. Our best financial consultants kept a book in which they wrote down customers who were interested in particular investments, such as municipal bonds, and then when the financial consultants got a new bond, they would pull out their book and start calling. We wanted to automate this process to create an online 'broker's book,' whereby financial consultants would receive automatic reminders to call customers about certain investment opportunities."

Perhaps most important to its vision of having a multichannel support system, Quick & Reilly needed to synchronize communication between its customers, financial consultants, customer resource center, and Web site. Without this synchronization, Quick & Reilly was unable to provide seamless customer support across all channels. When a customer or prospect called a financial consultant, the financial consultant had no way of knowing whether the customer had recently visited the Quick & Reilly Web site or spoken to a Quick & Reilly customer resource center agent. Similarly, if a customer called the Quick & Reilly customer resource center, the agent had no way of knowing if the customer had recently spoken to a personal financial consultant. The company needed an eBusiness system that would consolidate all customer data, including records of purchases, service requests, and other interactions, in a single repository and make that information available to all channels simultaneously.

Implementing a Multichannel eBusiness Solution

Quick & Reilly began the implementation of its eBusiness system in 1999. Dubbed "Socrates," the system serves as the core of the financial consultants's workstation. It provides the company's 1,200 financial consultants with a comprehensive view of its investors, along with key market information, and allows them to develop investment strategies to best meet customer needs. Financial consultants use the system's profiling tool to view information about investors, such as income and investment preferences, and target their investment pitches accordingly. The company is also able to reduce paperwork and make its financial consultants and service agents more efficient by putting key information—including promotional materials and company literature—at their fingertips. Moreover, the system assists management in analyzing where leads are coming from and determining which financial consultants are most productive.

"We are able to be so much more personal in our interactions now," explains Garry. "With essential customer information right in front of them, our representatives are able to develop customized investment strategies and deliver them—along with every appropriate piece of marketing collateral—directly to the customer, right from their desks. With nothing more than a mouse click, our third-party fulfillment house will send the appropriate marketing materials right to the customer." Quick adds that these more targeted and personalized interactions are critical to maintaining a competitive advantage. "To remain competitive, we have to be a lot smarter in spending resources to attract the best possible clients—those that are high-volume traders avail themselves of margin lending and keep cash balances in their accounts," he says. "Our eBusiness system helps us to be much more efficient and targeted in the way we attract and retain these investors."

Socrates also supports the delivery of a superior customer experience when customers visit the Quick & Reilly Web site or call the company's customer resource center. Customers can open an account on the Web site in one easy step and return anytime to manage that account. They can request information by sending e-mail to the customer resource center or engage in a real-time "Live Help Desk" discussion with a service agent via a Web chat. Each of the customer's interactions is documented within Quick & Reilly's eBusiness system, enabling the company's customer-facing employees to service customers much more efficiently, because they can see the customer's full history.

The consolidated pool of customer data serves as a valuable tool for acquiring new clients as well. "Our system now works in such an integrated fashion that no matter how a customer inquires about Quick & Reilly— whether on the Web, via an 800 number, by e-mail—his information automatically gets directed to a personal financial consultant, who then calls to follow up," says Quick. "The financial consultant asks some profiling questions and then captures information on the customer in his book as either someone to call on a regular basis if the customer is seeking financial advice, or someone to simply call occasionally if the customer would like to use the Internet or customer resource center as his main channel for trading. Either way, the customer knows that he has a personal financial consultant assigned to him if he should ever need help. Reaching out to the customer in this way at the very beginning solidifies the relationship. In fact, our conversion rate from initial inquiry to opening up an account has increased 20 percent since we implemented the eBusiness system."

Quick & Reilly has also derived benefits from tying its eBusiness system into US Clearing's recently deployed eBusiness system. Quick & Reilly has built performance metrics into its eBusiness system that enable it to set criteria for the length of time needed to handle various requests. If US Clearing ever goes beyond the time limit, the system sends the request directly to a supervisor. "The eBusiness system has enhanced our workflow," says Garry, "which allows us to set performance standards for our clearinghouse to ensure that our customers are being served properly."

Integration with FleetBoston Financial

Quick & Reilly management recognizes that consumers are increasingly looking for one-stop-shop financial services and has therefore begun to offer a broader array of services to its customers through its partnership with its parent company, FleetBoston Financial. "We know we're not the only game in town, so we need to position Quick & Reilly more as a provider of comprehensive financial products and services," says Quick. "That's critical to our future success." Quick & Reilly is working with Fleet to marry the companies' investment and banking offerings and cross-sell the products to both customer bases. All of Fleet's financial consultants have now become part of Quick & Reilly and are able to obtain leads from the Fleet Retail Bank operation. "Before, Fleet financial advisers were only able to offer a select number of investment products, but Fleet customers wanted more variety and depth in their investment options," explains Garry. "Meanwhile, Quick & Reilly customers wanted what Fleet offered—people who can come to your home and serve as a financial adviser. We've married those two businesses together to provide the best of both worlds."

As a result, customers are able to purchase a broad range of banking and investment services—from mortgages to mutual funds—from Quick & Reilly's brokerage offices, Web site, or customer resource center, or from any branch of Fleet Bank. The convergence of services between the two companies has been facilitated by Fleet's own implementation of our eBusiness applications. "Fleet has developed a very sophisticated system in its service centers that allows it to create a unified view of customer interactions and product purchases," says Garry. "Our shared focus on the customer enables us to work well together to provide the full array of products that customers need to fulfill all of their financial needs."

Currently, less than 10 percent of Fleet's customers use Quick & Reilly brokerage services. However, that percentage is expected to increase as the convergence of the two companies progresses. "We would like 100 percent of Fleet's customers to use our brokerage services," says Garry. "We want to become the one-stop shop for customers, whether they want banking services, mortgage services, small business services, or brokerage services. We want to make it so attractive to do business with Quick & Reilly that there is no need for them to go anywhere else. To this end, we are working with Fleet to cross-sell credit and ATM cards to our customers that allow them to make charges directly against their asset-management accounts."

Positioned for the Future

With its eBusiness system deployed, Quick & Reilly now has the ability to provide its customers with a seamless experience across all channels. Customers can conduct business with Quick & Reilly over the Web, through its customer resource center, or with one of its personal financial consultants, knowing that all three channels will share a single view of the customer's profile and transaction history. Customers can thus choose their channel depending on their needs. They can use the Internet if they prefer a low-cost channel with no human interaction; they can choose the customer resource center if they would like personal assistance in placing trades, opening an account, or addressing questions; and they can use their assigned personal financial consultants for more detailed help and in-depth financial planning. Moreover, they can switch channels at any time if their needs change.

Quick believes that his company is prepared to handle whatever external or internal changes will influence the company in the future. "We now have the technological infrastructure in place to adapt quickly to our clients' needs, and that will allow us to differentiate our company in a highly competitive marketplace," he says. "With our key partners such as FleetBoston Financial and US Clearing using the same eBusiness applications as well, we're developing a tightly integrated network that will help us expand the choices for our clients, go after new business with a targeted approach, and provide customer support that truly sets Quick & Reilly apart in today's fiercely competitive financial services industry."

CHAPTER TWENTY-THREE

The eBusiness Imperative

In the not-too-distant future, there will be no distinction between business and eBusiness—organizations will have become eBusinesses or will have perished. In other words, eBusiness is not a matter of choice but a matter of survival. The new economy requires organizations to know their customers better, to personalize their interactions with customers, and to deliver the highest levels of customer satisfaction. As competition intensifies throughout the world—in the wake of more deregulation, globalization, and technological innovation—organizations increasingly will be driven to focus on satisfying their customers. Organizations that can execute against that requirement will succeed; those that cannot will fail.

As indicated by the experiences of the numerous organizations recounted throughout this book, the impact from eBusiness capabilities is real and concrete: throughout the world, eBusiness pioneers are reaping the rewards of their early investments in eBusiness technology and processes. Based on the trail blazed by these pioneers, the principles and methodology presented in this book provide a clear road map of the eBusiness transformation. Regardless of size or industry or geography, organizations can now leverage to their own benefit the experience of those early leaders. But there is no advantage in delay. On the contrary, the advantage will go to those organizations that most quickly implement multichannel eBusiness capabilities to create strong, long-lasting relationships with loyal, profitable customers. It is imperative, therefore, for organizations to take the initiative and act now.

1. *E-Business: Opportunities, Threats and Paper Tigers,* V. Frick, B. Gill, A. Lill, and K. Murphy, GartnerGroup Strategic Analysis Report, 12/27/99, p. 7.

2. Ibid.

3. "Trial by Fire," Nelson D. Schwartz, *Fortune,* 6/26/00.

4. This section draws on ideas presented in *The Loyalty Effect: The Hidden Source Behind Growth, Profits, and Lasting Value,* Frederick F. Reichheld, Boston: Harvard Business School Press, 1996.

5. Paragraph based on information in "The Well-Rounded Consumer," Jeff Sweat, *InformationWeek,* 4/10/00, p. 54.

6. *The Channel Advantage,* Timothy R. Furey and Lawrence G. Friedman, Boston: Butterworth-Heinemann, 1999.

7. Ibid.

8. Research presented by McKinsey & Company (director Rob Yanker and principal Corey Yulinsky) at Siebel MultiChannel Services Worldwide Meeting, Key Largo, Florida, 5/5/00.

9. "Williams-Sonoma's Multi-channel Marketing Leads to Niche Dominance," Frank Barnett and Sharan Barnett, *Direct Marketing,* March 1999, p. 41.

10. "Clicks & Mortar," Malcolm Gladwell, *The New Yorker,* 12/6/99.

11. "The New Sales Force," Malcolm Campbell, *Selling Power,* July/August 1999.

12. "Why Satisfied Customers Defect," Thomas O. Jones and W. Earl Sasser, Jr., *Harvard Business Review,* November/December 1995.

13. This section draws on ideas presented in *The Market-Driven Organization: Understanding, Attracting, and Keeping Valuable Customers,* George S. Day, New York: Free Press, 1999.

14. "E-Loyalty: Your Secret Weapon on the Web," Frederick Reichheld and Phil Schefter, *Harvard Business Review,* July–August 2000, p. 112.

15. "Suite Returns," by Elana Varon, *CIO* magazine, August 15, 2000, p. 4.

16. Ibid., p. 5.

17. Ibid., p. 2.

18. Honeywell 1999 Annual Report.

19. Values taken from GE.com (http://www.ge.com/news/podium_papers/ourvalues.htm).

20. "Customer Centricity," C. K. Prahalad, *Information Week,* 4/10/00.

21. "Taking Stock," *ComputerWorld,* 6/26/00.

22. http://www.quicken.com/investments/stats/?symbol=DOW

23. http://www.quicken.com/investments/stats/?symbol=DD

24. Calculated from Dow's 1999 Annual Report.

25. Adapted from "Chemical Attraction," by Shari Weiss, www.CIO.com, August 15, 2000, p. 1.

26. Ibid., p. 3.

27. "Producing Sustainable Competitive Advantage Through the Effective Management of People," Jeffrey Pfeffer, *The Academy of Management Executive,* February 1995, Vol. 9, No. 1.

ACKNOWLEDGMENTS

This book would not have been possible without the support and contribution of many people. Special thanks goes to the customers of Siebel Systems for their generosity in sharing their experiences in the pages of this book. I regard it as an honor and a privilege that these organizations have placed their trust in Siebel Systems. Particular mention must be made of the individuals who gave their time and energy to be interviewed for the eBusiness leader profiles throughout the book (in alphabetical order by company name and individual name): Jim Burns, Denis O'Leary, Bruce Zimmerman (Chase Manhattan); Mack Murrell (Dow Chemical); Rob Baxter (Honeywell International, Inc.); Doug Maine (IBM); Mike Dalton (Marriott International); George McKinnon (Nationwide Insurance); Ed Garry, Tom Quick (Quick & Reilly); Peter Frueh, Negba M. Weiss-Dolev (Telstra); Dave Carter, Phil Goffin (Threadneedle Investments); Becky Christoff, Tom Kosko, Eloise McNeal (WorldCom). Additional thanks goes to Professor V. Kasturi Rangan of Harvard Business School and to Frank V. Cespedes of the Center for Executive Development for their comments on an early draft of the book. Thanks also to the many Siebel Systems employees and business partners who provided valuable input and assistance during the research and writing of this book.

THOMAS M. SIEBEL is the cofounder and CEO of Siebel Systems. The coauthor of *Cyber Rules*, he has been named one of the top executives of the year by *Business Week* and was number three on *Upside* magazine's "Elite 100."